THE
CONGRUENT LEADER

THE
CONGRUENT
LEADER

Build Trust, Lead with

Self-Awareness, and Close the Gap

Between How You See Yourself and

How Others Experience You

LeAnne Lagasse

THE CONGRUENT LEADER: Build Trust, Lead with Self-Awareness, and Close the Gap Between How You See Yourself and How Others Experience You

Copyright ©2025 by LeAnne Lagasse

Published by LeAnne Lagasse, White Mountain Stories

All Rights Reserved by White Mountain Stories, including the right of reproduction in whole or in part in any form. No part of this publication may be produced, stored in a retrieval system, or transmitted in any other form or by any means, electronic, mechanical, photocopying, recording, or otherwise, without the publisher's prior permission.

Neither the author nor the publisher will bear any responsibility or liability for any action taken by any person, persons or organization on the purported basis of information contained herein.

Without limiting the generality of the foregoing, no person, persons, or organization should take any action on reliance of the material contained herein. Instead, they should satisfy themselves independently (whether by expert advice or otherwise) of the appropriateness of such action.

Contact the publisher at: LeAnne@LeAnneLagasse.com

First edition, 2025

ISBN: 979-8-9995019-1-2 (Hard cover)
ISBN: 979-8-9995019-0-5 (Paperback)
ISBN: 979-8-9995019-2-9 (eBook)

Library of Congress Control Number: 2025919948

Editing by Deborah Ager | Radiant Media Labs
www.RadiantMediaLabs.com

Proofreading by Vanessa Boeser | Vanessa May Co

Cover design and interior formatting by Becky's Graphic Design®, LLC
www.BeckysGraphicDesign.com

To leaders who care deeply about how others experience them, who are brave enough to grow, humble enough to listen, and committed enough to change.

And to my children, Isaac, Eli, and Abby—may you always lead with strength, curiosity, and compassion, and never lose sight of the impact you have on others. Thanks for being my favorite (and most honest) feedback loop.

SELF-AWARENESS ALIG
STRENGTHS LIMITAT
PERCEPTION
OTHER-AWARENESS LE
SELF-AWARENESS ALIG
STRENGTHS LIMITAT
PERCEPTIONS OTHER-A
LEGACY SELF-AWA
ALIGNMENT STRE
LIMITATIONS PERCE
OTHER-AWARENESS LE
SELF-AWARENESS ALIGN
LIMITATIONS PERCE
OTHER AWARENESS LE
SELF-AWARE
ALIGNMENT STR
LIMITATIONS PERCEPT
OTHER-AWAREN
LEGACY SELF-AWAR

Contents

A Note on Stories and Identities 1

Resources to Help You Apply What You Learn 3

Introduction 5

1   Know Thyself: Why Self-Awareness Is the First Step to Better Leadership Outcomes.................13

2   Self-Concept: The Foundation of Congruent Leadership...35

3   Pursue Self-Awareness with Courage and Commitment...65

4   Bring Your Motivations, Values, and Actions into Alignment 85

5   Leverage Your Talents and Strengths 111

6   Manage Your Talent Gaps, Weaknesses, and Blind Spots 147

7   Respect the Collective Perception.................. 187

8   See and Lead People as They Are................... 219

9   Own Your Impact and Leadership Legacy.......... 255

Notes... 267

Bibliography 271

Acknowledgments 275

About the Author..................................... 277

Bring Congruent Leadership to Your Organization . 279

SELF-AWARENESS ALIGN
STRENGTHS LIMITAT
PERCEPTION
OTHER-AWARENESS LE
SELF-AWARENESS ALIG
STRENGTHS LIMITAT
PERCEPTIONS OTHER-A
LEGACY SELF-AWAR
ALIGNMENT STREN
LIMITATIONS PERCE
OTHER-AWARENESS LE
SELF-AWARENESS ALIGN
LIMITATIONS PERCE
OTHER AWARENESS LE
SELF-AWARE
ALIGNMENT STR
LIMITATIONS PERCEPT
OTHER-AWAREN
LEGACY SELF-AWAR

A Note on Stories and Identities

To honor the privacy and confidentiality of the individuals and organizations I've worked with, some names, identifying details, and circumstances in the stories throughout this book have been changed or adapted. While the core truths and lessons remain intact, these small shifts ensure that the focus stays on the learning, not their identities. My intention is always to protect trust while sharing real, meaningful leadership insights.

SELF-AWARENESS ALIGN
STRENGTHS LIMITAT
PERCEPTION
OTHER-AWARENESS LE
SELF-AWARENESS ALIG
STRENGTHS LIMITAT
PERCEPTIONS OTHER-A
LEGACY SELF-AWAR
ALIGNMENT STREN
LIMITATIONS PERCE
OTHER-AWARENESS LE
SELF-AWARENESS ALIGN
LIMITATIONS PERCE
OTHER AWARENESS LE
SELF-AWARE
ALIGNMENT STR
LIMITATIONS PERCEPT
OTHER-AWAREN
LEGACY SELF-AWAR

Resources to Help You Apply What You Learn

I know that work like this—deepening your self-awareness and aligning your leadership—takes time, reflection, and intention. I want you to get the most out of this experience, so I've created additional resources to help you along the way. At TheCongruentLeaderBook.com, you'll find reflection guides, conversation starters, and practical tools designed to help you apply the ideas from *The Congruent Leader* to your leadership, whether you're working through this book on your own, with a coach, or alongside your leadership team.

SELF-AWARENESS ALIG
STRENGTHS LIMITAT
PERCEPTION
OTHER-AWARENESS LE
SELF-AWARENESS ALIG
STRENGTHS LIMITAT
PERCEPTIONS OTHER-A
LEGACY SELF-AWA
ALIGNMENT STRE
LIMITATIONS PERCE
OTHER-AWARENESS LE
SELF-AWARENESS ALIGN
LIMITATIONS PERCE
OTHER AWARENESS LI
SELF-AWARE
ALIGNMENT STR
LIMITATIONS PERCEPT
OTHER-AWAREN
LEGACY SELF-AWA

Introduction

I DON'T KNOW PRECISELY why you, as a unique person, decided to read this book, and that frustrates me a bit. Let me explain. For as long as I can remember, I've been curious about the uniqueness of people and asked myself the following questions about others:

- "What makes this person tick?"
- "Why did they respond that way?"
- "What patterns can I spot in their behavior?"

As a child, my mom nicknamed me "The Nose" because I asked so many probing questions about others and listened into conversations I wasn't a part of. I was hungry to hone my people-watching skills any chance I could.

So, it's no surprise that, as a college student, I studied communication and psychology and was *that* student reading my textbooks for fun. I went on to earn a graduate degree in communication, where I also discovered a passion for teaching. After being hired as a faculty member and director at a public university in Texas, I suddenly found myself responsible for training and leading a large staff. Suffice it to say, I was a hot mess.

More on that later. For now, I'll just share that I was grossly underprepared for how much I would have to learn about myself and others to get the outcomes I needed in my leadership role.

Thankfully, I started to figure it out when I aimed my investigative people-watching skills at *myself*. That sounds odd, right? However, learning how to leverage my strengths, managing around my weaknesses, and understanding how others experienced me at work was a game-changer for me and the team members I led.

When I combined what I was learning about myself with my background in communication and my curiosity about people's uniqueness, I started to hit my stride. I was thriving and flourishing. More importantly, my team members also thrived and flourished.

After fourteen years in higher education, I left a stable and fulfilling career to chase a dream of owning a consulting, training, and coaching business where I could equip leaders and organizations to use the science of people and excellent communication skills to build an exceptional employee experience.

Basically, I'm a professional people-watcher now. I'm driven to explore the depths of what makes each leader I serve unique and distinct so that they can enjoy their leadership roles and build highly engaged and cohesive teams.

But back to the frustrating thing.

One of the most challenging parts of writing this book was knowing that I couldn't fully understand your unique context, strengths and weaknesses, challenges, or experiences as you read these pages. When I started this writing process, people asked me questions like, "Who is your ideal reader?" or "What do they need to learn from your book?" When I heard those questions, I felt frozen by uncertainty and lost in hesitation.

These generalized questions have always been complex for me to answer because, at my core, I believe that every leader I equip, train, or coach is unique. I struggle to synthesize the collective need of "my reader" because I naturally see every person based on what makes them different from every other person on the planet. This is one of my greatest strengths, but it gets in my way too.

All I knew was that "my reader" would come to the table with specific needs, wants, circumstances, and growth opportunities. So, I didn't write this book for one type of person. I wrote this book in a way that will hopefully resonate with each distinct person who picks it up.

Including you.

If I could, I'd love to sit down with you over coffee and learn more about you and your story. I genuinely believe your path to better leadership is as unique as you are. Because of that, I've written this book as an invitation to explore your own path of growth rather than giving you a one-size-fits-all formula. I dislike cookie-cutter advice, and I hope the tools and reflections here will help you discover the insights that matter most to you.

So, I think it's best if we start from the beginning.

"Why did you pick up this book?"

Perhaps you're feeling discouraged because your leadership experience isn't going as you hoped or expected. Or maybe you've received tough feedback recently—feedback that caught you off guard or made you question if you're cut out for leadership at all. Or what if, despite your best efforts, your team isn't responding well to your methods and you're not getting the outcomes you want and need in your leadership role? You might be feeling frustrated, discouraged, or insecure. You might be unsure why things aren't going the way you envisioned. Or perhaps you picked up this book because you're a leader driven by a deep desire to learn and grow, always looking for ways to improve your skills and build stronger connections with your team. You might even be reading this on someone else's recommendation, unsure if it's truly necessary for you.

Whatever your starting point, I want to invite you into this process of self-discovery with an open mind and heart. And I want you to know that you're not alone. Leadership is hard, and feeling uncertain or out of sync with yourself and your team is common. No matter how experienced, every leader faces moments of doubt where you wonder if you're missing something essential about yourself or your team. These moments of misalignment, where your intentions don't match the results you're getting, can make you question your leadership altogether.

At the heart of this book is the theme and goal of congruent leadership, which is the alignment between your internal self-concept and how others experience your leadership. Congruent leadership is more than self-knowledge, though, and involves adjusting and aligning to others' experiences, which leads to trust-building, higher engagement, and better performance. Along the way, you'll discover your strengths, uncover the blind spots holding you back, learn how to navigate difficult feedback, and discover new ways to connect with your team on a deeper, more meaningful level. It's a journey of growth and improvement, and the potential for transformation is within your reach if you're courageous and committed.

While most leaders believe they see themselves and others clearly, research shows self-awareness is rare, and that gap is where many leadership challenges begin. Without a clear understanding of who we are and how others perceive us, it's nearly impossible to build the kind of trust and connection that drives performance and engagement.

I built this book around seven core pillars that support congruent leadership. We'll explore them in more detail soon but, for now, here's what you can expect.

INTRODUCTION

We'll begin by looking inward:

- exploring our self-perception and mindset,
- uncovering our core motivations and values,
- identifying our natural talents,
- getting honest about the weaknesses and blind spots that might stand in the way, and
- moving toward feedback from others.

Then, we'll turn outward:

- Respecting others' perceptions and experiences of us,
- learning to see others clearly, and
- owning our impact and legacy.

Self-awareness extends beyond personal insight and into how you see and lead others. As the chapters unfold, you'll deepen your understanding of feedback, perception, bias, and the powerful impact of truly seeing people as they are. You'll learn how to individualize your leadership, communicate with greater trust and clarity, and ultimately own the impact and legacy you're creating through everyday choices. These seven pillars are here to be your guide, helping you lead with more clarity, humility, and intention, starting right where you are. In particular, we'll focus on four critical tools: curiosity, presence, self-disclosure, and individualization. These tools will help you make your team members feel truly seen and valued, which is at the heart of building trust and driving engagement. We'll conclude by exploring the leadership legacy you want to leave behind.

Through my work as a consultant and executive coach, I've had the privilege of helping leaders across industries develop these critical skills. My background in communication and psychology has allowed me to study the intricate ways in which leaders' perceptions of themselves often differ from those of their teams. What I've found is that leadership is based on how others experience you and not only about what you know or do. And that experience starts with understanding yourself and others with greater clarity.

While I believe you will find this process enjoyable, insightful, and even fun, the journey won't be easy. Real growth never is. Confronting ourselves can be uncomfortable and even painful, but I can promise you that it's worth it. When you commit to understanding yourself more deeply and seeing others more clearly, you unlock the potential for meaningful connections, stronger teams, and better outcomes. Whether you're here to address a specific issue or simply to become the best leader you can be, the tools and insights in this book will help you navigate the complexities of leadership with greater alignment and clarity.

As you read, I invite you to stay curious about yourself *and* others. Every leadership challenge you face is an opportunity to learn something new about yourself or the people you lead. Be open to what you discover, and know that this process will serve you well for the rest of your leadership career.

And while it's true that I don't know exactly why you are reading this book, I do know one thing for sure. You deserve to feel seen, known, valued, and developed, not just by others but also by yourself. Let's make it happen.

Just one more thing. Because I believe your growth journey is personal and unique, I've created a supplemental space where you can go deeper with the ideas in this book. At www.TheCongruentLeaderBook.com, you'll find downloadable

INTRODUCTION

exercises not included in these pages, a fillable journal with the Reflection Questions from each chapter, and other practical tools to help you apply what you're learning in your own leadership context.

This is one more way I'm cheering you on in this process and making sure you have the support you need as you grow.

Let's make it happen.

SELF-AWARENESS ALIGN
STRENGTHS LIMITAT
PERCEPTION
OTHER-AWARENESS LEG
SELF-AWARENESS ALIG
STRENGTHS LIMITAT
PERCEPTIONS OTHER-A
LEGACY SELF-AWAR
ALIGNMENT STREN
LIMITATIONS PERCE
OTHER-AWARENESS LE
SELF-AWARENESS ALIGNM
LIMITATIONS PERCE
OTHER AWARENESS LE
SELF-AWARE
ALIGNMENT STR
LIMITATIONS PERCEPT
OTHER-AWAREN
LEGACY SELF-AWAR

CHAPTER 1

Know Thyself: Why Self-Awareness Is the First Step to Better Leadership Outcomes

Key Question: *How might a clear understanding of how you see yourself, and how others experience you, transform your leadership impact?*

"WHAT IS YOUR BIGGEST *barrier or greatest challenge when it comes to getting good outcomes as a leader?"*

This is one of my favorite questions to ask leaders, and over the years, I've asked it countless times during team workshops, corporate training events, and one-on-one leadership coaching sessions. Leaders often speak up with common and relatable answers, such as "poor communication," "organizational silos," "poor performance," or the all too familiar, "unmotivated and disengaged employees."

I don't disagree, by the way. All of these answers are legitimate, yet it's noteworthy that in all my years of asking this question, not once has a leader responded with something resembling, "Me. I'm part of the problem."

Now, that's not to say there aren't leaders out there who sense they are the biggest barrier to their own success. In fact, when writing this chapter introduction, I wondered how many of you might say precisely that based on the fact that you picked up the book in the first place. The takeaway is that, as leaders, we are less likely to see ourselves as the starting point for solving our biggest challenges and problems. We're much more likely to seek out the best strategies, tools, and resources and bypass the introspection and reflection that would yield tremendous insight into the problem and help us identify the best solutions. Introspection, or the act of looking inward, is a crucial part of leadership development that is often overlooked.

The idea of turning inward to lead better isn't new. In fact, the ancient Greek maxim "Know thyself" was inscribed at the Temple of Apollo at Delphi and later championed by Socrates, as recorded by Plato. This maxim has echoed through centuries of philosophy and psychology as the starting point for wisdom. And for leaders today, it's still one of the most important underrated and overlooked starting points for transformation.

I often speak with leaders at the top of an organizational chart who reach out to me and assume the solution to their most significant organizational challenges lies in finding the perfect training, workshop, or curriculum to motivate others.

It's rare (read: never) that a leader calls and says, "We've got some big problems with our work culture. We're not getting the outcomes we need, and we're pretty sure we're to blame at the top."

So much leadership development content falls flat because the solutions focus solely on external strategies, on getting others to fall in line, motivating teams, or driving buy-in for change. These are important goals, to be sure, but they often miss a crucial component: an exploration of the leader's internal landscape. That's a shame because our mindsets and how we see ourselves directly influence how we lead, how others experience our leadership, and, ultimately, the outcomes we achieve.

Consider Rachelle, a mid-level leader in a nonprofit organization, who struggles with a crippling amount of self-doubt about her leadership competency. She sees herself as inexperienced and unworthy of her position, even though she has a track record of success, including leading a community engagement campaign that exceeded its fundraising goal by 40 percent and mentoring two team members into more senior roles.

Despite these achievements, Rachelle's insecurity shows up in her daily interactions. In team meetings, she often starts her sentences with "This might be a bad idea, but..." or "You all probably know better than I do....." She frequently revisits decisions she's already made, such as changing timelines on projects or reassigning responsibilities after she's delegated them, not because of new information, but because she's second-guessing herself. Team members have noticed her asking, "Is that okay?" or "What do you think?" even on matters well within her authority to decide.

When a major funding proposal falls through due to shifting priorities from the granting organization, Rachelle immediately assumes full blame. In a team meeting, she opens with, "This is completely my fault" despite the team having followed all the guidelines and timelines precisely. Rather than analyzing what could be learned from the experience of helping the team move forward, Rachelle's focus on personal fault casts a shadow over the group's morale. Team members begin to question her ability to lead, not because she lacks skill or insight, but because her self-doubt projects uncertainty and instability. They hesitate to bring ideas forward or make autonomous decisions, unsure whether their contributions will be second-guessed or over-apologized for later.

Rachelle's story illustrates how a leader's self-concept can significantly shape outcomes. Without the ability to see ourselves clearly and reflect on how others experience us, we risk a critical misalignment between our intentions and our impact—a gap that can erode trust, hinder progress, and stifle growth.

Here's a statistic I share with anyone who will listen: According to the Gallup Organization, about 70 percent of what drives employee engagement comes down to one thing: the people manager.[1] That's a staggering figure, and it highlights how deeply a leader's behavior, mindset, and self-awareness influence team dynamics.

This raises the question: What if the solution to our biggest leadership problems is uncovering the truth about ourselves and how we show up when problems arise instead of trying to "fix" other people?

Think about the challenges you're currently facing in your leadership role. Are you struggling with any of the following?

- Experiencing conflict on your team.

- Feeling overwhelmed with your workload.

- Having trouble motivating your team members to chase after your team mission.

- Dealing with resistance to change, lack of team cohesion, or difficulty in managing remote teams.

All of the above are common challenges that leaders face, and it would be easy to diagnose the issues as being outside of our own actions, thoughts, and behaviors. For a few of the challenges listed above, we might tell ourselves, "This conflict wouldn't happen if it weren't for that one team member," or "No one knows how hard I'm working behind the scenes," or "This younger generation of employees just doesn't have a strong work ethic."

Again, there might be some truth to these thoughts. That's not the point. The point is that to be self-aware and authentic leaders, we must always tackle our challenges by looking inward first.

That raises another question: What if the *answer* to our greatest leadership challenges lies in our response to the following questions: "How do I *see* myself compared to how others *experience* me?" and "How can I align my internal beliefs, values, and self-perception to match my external actions, communication, and impact on others?"

Please give yourself a moment to pause and reflect on these questions. I don't intend for them to be hypothetical. But if you're like the vast majority of leaders, you probably assume you're already pretty self-aware. But research, and our real-world experience, suggests otherwise. According to organizational psychologist and self-awareness researcher Dr. Tasha Eurich, while most people believe they're self-aware, only about 10 to 15 percent actually are.[2] As it turns out, we humans are great at overestimating ourselves and our abilities.

I don't share this to lead you into despair or shame. I share this because if it's true that we're not as self-aware as we think we are, and the research suggests that's the case for at least 85 percent of us, we must approach our leadership with a healthy amount of skepticism and curiosity. Not the kind that makes us insecure but the kind that keeps us grounded and humbled about the impact we have on those around us.

Self-awareness is a lifelong pursuit, and we must bring courage and curiosity along for the ride.

A lack of self-awareness might look like a leader who believes they're approachable and open to ideas but constantly interrupts their team, inadvertently stifling innovation. Or it might show up in a leader who values fairness but unknowingly plays favorites, eroding trust among their team members. These disconnects create ripple effects, undermining morale, trust, and productivity.

Let's remember that struggling with self-awareness doesn't make us bad leaders. Instead, it makes us human. Self-awareness is a lifelong pursuit, and we must bring courage and curiosity along for the ride. The fact that you're reading this book already places you ahead of most leaders in recognizing the importance of self-awareness.

In the rest of this chapter, we'll explore how self-awareness impacts leadership outcomes, identify the common signs and costs of low self-awareness, and provide practical tools to uncover blind spots, align intentions with actions, and build trust with your team.

REFLECTION QUESTIONS

Have you ever been caught off guard by feedback that didn't match how you see yourself? If so, what surprised you?

_____

_____

_____

Have you found that your team isn't responding to your leadership the way you hoped, despite your best intentions? How so?

_____

_____

_____

What might this reveal about the gap between your intentions and how others experience you?

_____

_____

_____

What Is Self-Awareness?

Self-awareness is "the ability to see ourselves clearly—to understand who we are, how others see us, and how we fit into the world."
—DR. TASHA EURICH, AUTHOR OF *INSIGHT* [3]

Self-awareness is a word that gets thrown around a lot, mostly to point out when someone does not possess it. But what is it exactly?

I've found that people generally find it easier to describe the effects of a lack of self-awareness than to define the concept itself. One workshop attendee made everyone laugh and nod in agreement when he shouted from the back of the room, "I don't know how to define it exactly, but I know it when I see it and when I don't see it."

Isn't that about right? Sometimes, it's easier to understand a concept when considering what it isn't.

What comes to mind when you think of someone with low self-awareness? Maybe it's a leader who claims to be approachable but shuts down every new idea. Or someone who views themselves as decisive but leaves their team confused with mixed messages. Perhaps someone with a very high view of themselves, but behind their back, everyone around the office makes fun of them for their incompetence.

And what comes to mind when you think of someone with high self-awareness? Maybe it's a leader who actively seeks feedback and adjusts their approach based on the needs of their team. Or someone who remains calm and measured under pressure, recognizing how their emotional responses could influence others. Perhaps it's a leader who knows their strengths and uses them to inspire and guide their team while also being honest and humble about their blind spots, empowering others to step in and fill the gaps. High self-awareness in leaders often shows up as consistency, adaptability, and the ability to build trust through genuine alignment between their intentions and actions.

Shelley Duval and Robert Wicklund were trailblazers in self-awareness research, introducing *Self-Awareness Theory* in the early 1970s.[4] Their work highlighted the pivotal role of self-focused attention in helping individuals align their behavior with internal standards, setting the stage for decades of research on personal growth and leadership development.

I've already mentioned her once before, but one of my favorite self-awareness researchers and the author of *Insight*, Dr. Tasha Eurich, defines self-awareness as our ability to see ourselves clearly—both internally and in terms of how others see us and how we show up in the world. Dr. Eurich makes a compelling case, which I agree with wholeheartedly, that self-awareness is the meta-skill of the twenty-first century.

Another of my favorites, Daniel Goleman, a psychologist and renowned author of *Emotional Intelligence*, is widely recognized for popularizing the concept of emotional intelligence in leadership. He defines self-awareness as "self-reflexive, introspective attention to one's own experience."[5] Goleman emphasizes that this awareness isn't just about introspection; it's about recognizing how our emotions shape not only our own responses but also the emotional climate around us. According to Goleman, self-awareness begins with self-recognition, the understanding that our inner world directly impacts how we lead, how others feel around us, and the outcomes we create together.[6]

At root, self-awareness is our ability to understand our

internal selves—our values, motivations, emotions, and behavior—and our external impact: how others perceive and experience us.

What Does Self-Awareness Afford Us?

My hunch is that I probably don't need to spend much time convincing you that self-aware leaders are rated more favorably than leaders with low self-awareness or that research shows that leaders with strong self-awareness tend to be more effective in their roles, better at empathizing with others, and more successful at motivating and inspiring their teams to reach higher levels of performance.[7] But I'm going to do it anyway, because I'm a fan of citing my sources.

Decades of research confirms what many of us have experienced intuitively: Self-aware leaders consistently outperform their less self-aware peers. In fact, Showry, et al., cited a survey by Stanford which identified self-awareness as one of the most critical soft skills for effective leadership, predicting both managerial effectiveness and leadership success.[8] As noted by Bennis, Goleman, O'Toole, and Biederman, leaders who demonstrate high self-awareness not only make better and more informed decisions—by managing emotional triggers and cognitive biases—they also foster stronger, more trusting relationships with their teams and are able to consider multiple perspectives before acting.[9] In case you needed more evidence, Gross and John found that self-aware leaders are better at regulating emotions, helping them maintain a positive influence during challenging times, particularly under stress.[10]

Self-aware leaders tend to enjoy better work relationships, experience less stress, and engage in more thoughtful, reflective leadership practices. In short, self-awareness makes you a more impactful leader. Again, I bet you've likely experienced firsthand that self-aware leaders are:

- Genuine and transparent about who they are and who they aren't;
- Mindful of the impact their behaviors and emotions have on others;
- Open to feedback, actively seeking it, and adapting based on it;
- Approachable, fostering psychological safety within their teams;
- Better equipped to build stronger interpersonal relationships;
- More trusted because their actions align with their values.

Self-aware leaders achieve better outcomes, build stronger reputations, and make a more significant impact. Sounds great, doesn't it?

And Now, Some Concerning News

We've already learned that we're probably not as self-aware as we think. Perhaps we've come to terms with that and are humble and curious enough to explore the gap between how we see ourselves and how others experience us.

Even still, many leaders I work with underestimate how susceptible we are to becoming delusional about ourselves, our abilities, and our areas of strength. Even formerly self-aware leaders tend to become less self-aware over time.

The *Dunning-Kruger effect* explains why leaders often overestimate their abilities.[11] This effect is a cognitive bias in which individuals with low competence in a specific area fail to recognize their deficiencies. This lack of self-awareness leads to inflated self-perceptions, as they lack the skills to accurately evaluate their performance. In leadership, this can manifest as overconfidence in decision-making, misjudging team dynamics, or dismissing feedback. Leaders affected by this bias may assume they're effective simply because they don't perceive their blind spots, making it critical to seek external feedback and reflect honestly on their impact to avoid the pitfalls of this effect.

Right now, I bet you're thinking of someone specific who fits this description, and you're probably right to do so. We're all susceptible to the Dunning-Kruger effect.

How about this? Would you be surprised to learn that, statistically, the most un-self-aware people in an organization are likely to be at the top of the org chart? While you might think more leadership experience would equate to better self-awareness, studies often show the opposite. Dr. Eurich says it this way:

"Contrary to popular belief, studies have shown that people do not always learn from experience, that expertise does not help people root out false information, and that seeing ourselves as highly experienced can keep us from doing our homework, seeking disconfirming evidence, and questioning our assumptions." How in the world does that happen?

On an individual level, a variety of contributing factors affects this. But, in general, two major reasons exist:

1. Leaders tend to receive less performance feedback than individual contributors. As you climb the leadership ladder, roles tend to become more ambiguous, making concrete feedback more elusive. Additionally, in most organizations, performance feedback primarily flows downward. Our entry-level employees often field the bulk of feedback.

2. Perhaps the more significant reason this happens is that,

as we grow in authority, status, and perceived power in our organization, people are less likely to tell us the truth about how they view us. The stakes for honest feedback are bigger for those who believe they have more to lose due to their lower organizational status.

Here's the main point. We tend to lose self-awareness over time because, as leaders, we tend to receive less frequent feedback and less honest feedback from others. Over time, the lack of honest feedback impacts our self-concept in ways we're unaware of, perpetuating the problem.

This erosion of self-awareness has tangible consequences that affect not just leaders but also the teams and organizations they lead. Without clear insight into how we're perceived, our actions can unintentionally create mistrust, hinder collaboration, and even sabotage our progress.

The Cost of Low Self-Awareness

If we don't see ourselves clearly, we'll face consequences that ripple through our teams and organizations, ultimately limiting our ability to achieve good outcomes and be the kind of leaders we want to be.

For starters, when there is a big gap between how we see ourselves and how others experience us, we will struggle to build trust and credibility with others. Trusting someone who cannot see their impact on others is difficult, if not near impossible in the workplace. It's also hard to trust someone who makes poor decisions due to unexamined biases, assumptions, or flawed judgments and strategies.

Speaking of trust, lacking self-awareness can make us appear tone-deaf to our team needs, leading to disengagement, decreased morale, and higher turnover. We'll likely struggle with misalignment, seeming out of touch with our teams' real challenges.

Have you ever been blindsided by a team member's frustration with you or a project outcome that didn't meet expectations despite your best efforts? These moments often stem from blind spots in how we perceive ourselves and how others experience us.

Interpersonally, such blind spots can hinder our ability to empathize and connect with others, weakening relationships and reducing team cohesion. Blind spots can also cause us to struggle with navigating or resolving conflicts because we fail to see how our behavior contributes to the problem.

Furthermore, failing to reflect on our behavior or the feedback we receive from others means we'll miss valuable opportunities to grow and mature as leaders, ultimately affecting our team's performance.

Research shows that an unaware person on a team reduces decision quality by an average of 36 percent, hurts coordination by 46 percent, and increases conflict by 30 percent.[12] Additionally, companies with a large number of unaware employees perform worse financially. For example, The Korn Ferry Institute analyzed nearly 7,000 self-assessments from professionals across 486 publicly traded companies, and researchers investigated discrepancies between how individuals rated their own leadership strengths and how their coworkers perceived those same skills—essentially identifying self-awareness "blind spots."[13] These blind spots occurred when professionals viewed certain skills as strengths. Meanwhile their colleagues viewed those same "skills" as weaknesses.

The researchers then compared the prevalence of these blind spots to each company's return on revenue (ROR). They found a clear pattern: Employees at companies with weaker financial performance exhibited 20 percent more blind spots and were 79 percent more likely to show low overall self-awareness, compared to their peers at companies with stronger financial returns.

This makes sense, doesn't it? A lack of self-awareness doesn't merely affect how others perceive you. The lack has negative implications for your reputation, career progression, and leadership impact. Leaders who fail to recognize how their behaviors and habits influence their teams risk undermining their credibility. For instance, a leader who constantly interrupts others in meetings may not realize that this habit erodes their reputation as a collaborator, making it harder for their ideas to gain traction. Similarly, a leader who reacts emotionally under stress might unintentionally create a culture of fear or hesitation among their team.

Understanding the costs of low self-awareness highlights why this skill is essential for effective leadership. But how do you know if self-awareness is an area where you struggle? As we've already discussed, while it's easy to spot a lack of self-awareness in others, recognizing it in ourselves is far more challenging. Let's explore the most common signs of low self-awareness to help you evaluate where you might have blind spots in your leadership.

Warning Signs of Low Self-Awareness in Leaders

A lack of self-awareness doesn't always announce itself loudly. Rather, it often shows up in subtle, day-to-day behaviors that slowly erode trust, team cohesion, and effectiveness. These warning signs can be easily overlooked, especially for leaders who haven't actively sought feedback or reflected on their actions. Recognizing these behaviors is the first step toward addressing them and developing the self-awareness necessary for effective leadership.

Here are some common ways low self-awareness manifests in leadership:

- **Avoiding or Fearing Feedback:** These leaders actively avoid soliciting feedback or are terrified of hearing something that confirms their worst suspicions about themselves. They often interpret criticism as a personal attack rather than a chance to grow. This fear creates blind spots and slows down development.

- **Dismissiveness Toward Feedback:** Leaders with low self-awareness often deflect or dismiss constructive criticism. They might respond defensively, shift blame, or disregard feedback entirely.

- **Overconfidence:** These leaders are blind to their weaknesses and assume their way is always right because of their skill, experience, competence, and so on. Imagine a leader undermining their authority by ignoring team input and assuming they know best when everyone in the office knows otherwise.

- **Insecurity:** Overly self-doubting leaders second-guess decisions, avoid risks, and create instability, leading to a lack of trust in their leadership. One leader I worked with was notorious for apologizing repeatedly, which ultimately led to her team wondering if she was up for the challenge of leadership.

- **Inconsistency Between Values and Actions:** These leaders often fail to "walk the talk." They might claim to value collaboration but dominate conversations or claim to support innovation while rejecting new ideas, causing credibility issues.

- **Over-Reliance on Strengths:** Leaders with low self-awareness often overuse their preferred methods or strengths, applying them to every situation even when they aren't appropriate. For example, a results-driven leader might push too hard on deadlines, neglecting team morale.

- **Mismanagement of Emotional Triggers:** These leaders might lash out under stress, withdraw under challenging situations, or allow their emotions to cloud judgment, creating a volatile environment.

I almost didn't want to include this section in the chapter because I fear we might look through this list and think we're in the clear. In fact, if you read that list and thought, *Oh no, I know someone like that*, take a breath because that person might be you. We must remember that we're probably not as self-aware as we think, and some of the above bullet points are probably relevant to us.

I'm sure all of these warning signs impact me somewhat, but the one that resonates the most is avoiding or fearing feedback. When I began teaching large undergraduate courses in my mid-twenties, I was overwhelmed by the anonymous and confidential feedback I received at the end of every semester. Around 1,000 students would fill out a form evaluating my teaching effectiveness and style. Reading through those comments took a lot of courage. I have often said that few people are meaner than an anonymous college student having to take a public speaking course.

Anyway, in a particularly stressful semester a few years in, I can remember receiving the email that my course evaluations were ready to view. Delete. I was not up for it.

It wasn't until three months later, when I had to access those evaluations for my annual performance review, that I finally read through the comments from that previous semester. I will never forget what I learned.

A curriculum decision I made that I thought was in the best interest of the students had the opposite effect. As I read through those comments, a clear theme emerged: "This policy is unfair, and thus, you are not treating us with respect by enforcing it."

I had no idea my curriculum decision was perceived this way. I wouldn't have anticipated that, and it wasn't my intention. The news of this perception was deeply upsetting because one of my deepest core values is fairness and consistency.

How did I miss this? I thought to myself. Then, it hit me. I was in the middle of another semester and operating under this same policy.

Had I found the courage and grit to move toward the feedback, as painful as it might have been at the time, I would have surely reevaluated the policy. If nothing else, I could have improved my communication about the policy to ensure students understood my intentions and the reasons for its inclusion in the course. But because of my avoidance and fear of the feedback, I missed an opportunity to build more trust with my students. My avoidance resulted in a lack of awareness that continued to haunt me, and I had no idea.

KNOW THYSELF

REFLECTION QUESTIONS

Are there areas where you've avoided or dismissed feedback, only to discover later that the information was critical for your growth?

_____

_____

_____

Of the common signs listed above, which do you think you are most susceptible to, and why? Can you think of a specific situation from your past that would serve as an example?

_____

_____

_____

What's one area where you suspect blind spots might be affecting your leadership?

_____

_____

_____

A Call to Self-Awareness and Congruent Leadership

Self-awareness is the first step toward building alignment between how you see yourself and how others experience your leadership. As a reminder, this alignment is what we call *leadership congruence*: the harmony between your internal values, beliefs, and self-perception, as well as your external behaviors, communication, and impact.

Understanding yourself is step one, but self-awareness alone isn't enough. In the next chapter, we'll explore how to align your self-perception with your external actions to create the trust and credibility that define congruent leadership.

CHAPTER 2

Self-Concept: The Foundation of Congruent Leadership

Key Question: *How clearly do you see yourself, and how might that perception shape your leadership outcomes?*

I ASKED MY THEN thirteen-year-old son, Isaac, to describe me in three words one evening after we finished eating dinner together. This is not something I would have ever thought to do or would have wanted to do, for that matter, but my counselor had assigned me homework to reach out to the twenty people closest to me and ask them this question. For some context, I was walking through a particularly painful season of my life. My business partnership had just dissolved, and I was grappling with a deep sense of failure and loss. Internally, I felt small, unsteady, unsure of myself for the first time in a long time—and utterly defeated.

The exercise sounded simple enough—ask friends and family for three words they'd use to describe me. My counselor framed this homework as a way to reconnect with my strengths and gain perspective on how others saw me. Because I'm a rule follower, I begrudgingly followed her instructions.

Most of the responses I received were affirming but predictable. Words like "hardworking," "insightful," and "resilient" showed up repeatedly. I wasn't surprised by those responses. Even if I didn't fully feel them in the season I was in, I could objectively acknowledge these qualities about myself.

But when Isaac handed me the sticky note where he wrote down the three words that came to his mind, I could have never anticipated the first word staring back at me.

The word he wrote was the last word I would have ever used to describe myself.

"Courageous."

I don't even remember the other two words he wrote down because they didn't stop me in my tracks like the first one did.

I stared at the paper for a minute and started weeping, which is a rare occurrence for me. Isaac was worried, to say the least. At that moment, I felt anything but courageous. If anything, I felt terrified—terrified of the unknown, terrified of starting over, and terrified of how I might rebuild my sense of identity after such a significant loss. How could anyone, let alone someone as close to me as my son, see courage when all I could feel was fear?

His words stayed with me, stirring something I hadn't realized about myself. Isaac wasn't basing his description on the feelings I carried internally. He was basing it on the actions he saw me take every day: the way I showed up for him and others, the way I made hard decisions about my business, and the way I kept moving forward, even when I felt paralyzed with fear.

That single word, "courageous," was a powerful mirror to my self-concept and showed me the gap between how I saw myself and how others likely experienced me. This exchange was a moment of profound clarity for me. My fractured self-concept wasn't the whole story.

With this realization, I began to do the hard work of examining how I saw myself. I started asking more questions, leaning into feedback, and exploring what was true versus what was simply my inner narrative. Through this process, I grew tremendously, not because I changed who I was, but because I finally started to see myself more clearly.

That experience taught me a powerful truth: Our self-concept is the foundation of how we show up in the world. When we take the time to explore and align it with the reality of how others experience us, we unlock the clarity and confidence to lead with greater authenticity and impact.

This is the essence of what we call congruent leadership, which is the whole point of this book. "Congruence" means, "agreement or harmony, or compatibility." *Leadership* congruence refers to aligning who we are on the inside—our beliefs, values, and self-concept—with the behaviors, actions, and communication that shape how others experience us. Though originally discussed in the context of healthcare leadership and research, David Stanley, of the University of New England in Australia, defines congruent leadership as when "the activities, actions, and deeds of the leader are matched by and driven by their values and beliefs."[14]

As we explored in chapter one, self-awareness is the gateway to this alignment and helps us understand both how we perceive ourselves and how others perceive us. Without self-awareness, we may unintentionally act in ways that contradict our intentions, creating a disconnect that undermines trust and authenticity. So, how do we achieve congruent leadership?

The process of becoming a congruent leader, which we'll discuss more at the end of this chapter and throughout the rest of the book, begins with understanding and exploring our self-concept—the foundation of how we think, feel, and act as leaders. In this chapter, we'll dive deeper into self-concept, how it forms, and how it serves as the foundation for congruent leadership. Then, we'll introduce the Seven Pillars of Congruent Leadership, which provide a road map for aligning your internal and external leadership presence.

But before we explore our self-concept, I want to address an objection others sometimes make to this book's premise. Because this is a hill I will die on.

Rethinking the "Think of Yourself Less" Leadership Philosophy

Well-intentioned leadership advice often encourages leaders to think of themselves less and focus on serving others instead. A keynote speaker at an event I attended once said to a group of young leaders: "Leadership is easy when you forget about yourself." I wanted to shout from the rooftops, "No, that's terrible advice!" On the surface, this advice seems noble. Yes, leaders should avoid self-centeredness, serve their teams, and prioritize others' needs. However, this advice oversimplifies a crucial truth: Great leadership starts with understanding yourself well and using that knowledge to work more meaningfully and effectively with others.

When we take the concept of "think of yourself less" too literally, we risk neglecting the self-awareness necessary for effective leadership. We can use it as a crutch to avoid examining ourselves for patterns of behavior or communication that create barriers for us and our team members. Conversely, thinking more accurately about ourselves—knowing our strengths, acknowledging our blind spots, and understanding our motivations—is responsible and not selfish.

Consider this: If leaders don't know what drives them, how can they inspire others? How can they address those gaps if they can't see where they fall short? Leaders who understand themselves deeply are better equipped to serve others because they bring clarity, stability, alignment, and intentionality to their actions.

So, instead of thinking of ourselves less, let's think more *accurately* about ourselves. The goal is not to become self-absorbed and puffed up about ourselves. Similarly, the goal is not to become so self-critical that we overthink every leadership decision. Instead, let's understand our strengths, acknowledge our blind spots, and embrace the growth process. Congruent leadership begins with clarity about who we are so that our team can depend on the consistency of our actions and values.

What Is Our Self-Concept?

Have you ever been surprised by how someone else sees you? Maybe they described you with a word or trait you'd never considered or couldn't believe applied to you. My son's unexpected description of me as "courageous" challenged how I saw myself and opened the door to deeper clarity about how I show up, despite my often self-defeating thoughts. That moment made me realize how much our self-concept shapes our choices, the risks we take, and how we lead.

So, what exactly is this self-concept of ours? How does it form, and how does it influence the alignment, or misalignment, between who we think we are and how others experience us? Psychologist Carl Rogers defined self-concept as the collection of beliefs and perceptions an individual holds about themselves, encompassing their roles, values, and abilities, essentially forming their understanding of "who they are" as a person.[15] These beliefs act as a lens through which we see the world and ourselves in it, shaping how we interpret feedback, set goals, and interact with others.

Our self-concept develops over time and is continually

shaped by internal reflection and external experiences, including the feedback we receive (or avoid) from others. For leaders, this can mean everything from how they define their success to how they react when their authority or ideas are challenged.

A leader's self-concept provides the foundation for decision-making, influencing what they prioritize and how they define success. For example, if you see yourself as collaborative, you may invest heavily in building consensus with your team for decisions of all types. Or if you view yourself as a decisive problem-solver, you may favor quick action over thoughtful deliberation, regardless of what the situation warrants. More on this later.

But here's where it gets tricky: As we've already established in chapter one, our self-concept isn't always accurate. Since it's shaped by past experiences, cultural expectations, and even the stories we tell ourselves about our strengths and weaknesses, a gap between how we see ourselves and how others experience us can create friction, misunderstandings, mistrust, and missed opportunities.

REFLECTION QUESTIONS

What words, values, or identities come to mind when you think about who you are in your leadership role and beyond?

_____

_____

_____

SELF-CONCEPT

How do you define yourself, and where do those definitions come from? Are they based on how you want to see yourself, how others have labeled you, or the realities of your actions?

_____

_____

_____

What happens when your perception of yourself doesn't align with how others experience your leadership? Do you recognize the disconnect, or does it go unnoticed?

_____

_____

_____

Understanding and exploring your self-concept is the first step toward bridging that gap and becoming a more congruent leader.

Since our self-concept is a combination of enduring *and* evolving views about ourselves, parts of our identities will feel firm and unshakeable while others feel less stable. This balance of consistency and fluidity can impact how we lead and how others experience us.

Self-concept clarity is the degree to which individuals have a clearly defined, consistent, and enduring sense of self.[16] Leaders with high self-concept clarity have a more clear and stable self-concept that endures over time, and they feel confident about who they are. Self-concept clarity has many advantages because it can empower us to make confident decisions, communicate authentically, and align our behavior with our core values. Additionally, it can build trust by ensuring that our behaviors remain predictable and steady, even in stressful situations. Leaders with high self-concept clarity inspire confidence and create a sense of stability for their teams, helping them to navigate challenges and set clear priorities.

It's worth noting that ambiguity in self-concept can have the opposite effect. Leaders who lack clarity about their identity and values often send mixed signals, leaving their teams uncertain about expectations or priorities. This indecision erodes trustworthiness and undermines team cohesion as followers struggle to align their work with a leader who appears inconsistent or unclear.

Lest we think that self-concept clarity is all advantage, a word of caution:

Overly rigid self-concepts—those that resist new insights, adaptation, or feedback—can hinder growth, blind leaders to new perspectives, and create barriers to effective leadership in dynamic environments.

The key is balancing clarity with the adaptability needed for evolving contexts. The first step in this process is to confront our self-concept head-on.

To get started, ask yourself the following questions:

- Do you feel confident explaining who you are and what you stand for?

- When you think about who you are, do you feel your sense of self is consistent across different areas of your life, or does it feel fragmented or situational?

Reflecting on the Influences That Shape Our Self-Concept

Countless internal and external influences shape our self-concept. From the feedback we receive from others to the comparisons we make and the beliefs we hold about ourselves, these factors continually shape, challenge, and refine how we see ourselves.

Below is a list of common influences that shape our self-concepts. Of course, this list isn't exhaustive, but it's a great place to start. As you consider each influence, I encourage you to pause and reflect on the questions I pose at the end of each section. These questions offer an opportunity to better understand how we arrive at the conclusions we make about ourselves and our leadership styles. Let's start by examining one of the most significant influences: how we compare ourselves to others.

Social Comparison

One of the most powerful ways we form our self-concept is through *social comparison*, which involves observing and assigning meaning to others' behavior and outcomes and comparing them with ours. Psychologist Leon Festinger (1954) is known for introducing *Social Comparison Theory*, which explains how we evaluate ourselves by comparing our abilities, achievements, and characteristics to those of others, especially those we want to emulate.[17]

We learn who we are and who we aren't, in part, by watching others closely. For example, I see myself today as a competent public speaker partly because I watched others struggle with the skill at an early age while it seemed to come naturally to me. Those early experiences shaped my self-concept and ultimately affected my career choices.

As leaders, we will likely measure ourselves against peers, mentors, and team members. In the early days of my teaching career, I often compared myself to one of my mentors, who was incredibly skilled at presenting to, and facilitating discussion among, many students. He made it look effortless, and watching him teach large lecture courses taught me more about my unique teaching style. I would ask myself, "Where are there overlaps between his strengths and mine, and where are there gaps where I'm not going to get the same outcomes he gets?" Specifically, by watching him, I discovered that he had a natural and instinctual talent for bringing humor and quirkiness into his lectures. Let's just say I did not get the same outcomes. That would be an understatement. If I got a laugh from students, it was an accident or because I did something weird. But by watching him closely, I learned who I was as a unique teacher. I had value to bring in other areas and, by leaning into that, I was better poised to become the teacher I wanted to be.

In another season of my life, however, I became fixated on comparing myself to someone I admired to the point that it derailed me from being who I authentically was. I share this as a reminder that the conclusions we draw from social comparisons aren't always accurate or helpful. While comparisons can motivate growth, they can also create insecurities or overconfidence if based on flawed or incomplete information. Understanding this dynamic is critical for us if we're seeking to develop a healthy and balanced self-concept.

REFLECTION QUESTIONS

Who have you compared yourself to most in your life, and how has that influenced how you see yourself today?

_____

_____

_____

What comparisons have motivated growth in your leadership journey, and which ones have held you back?

_____

_____

_____

The Looking-Glass Self

Another key influence on our self-concept is the *looking-glass self*, a concept introduced by sociologist Charles Cooley, which explores how we shape our identity based on how we believe others perceive and judge us.[18] In leadership, this concept takes on special significance, as feedback—whether explicit or subtle—acts as a mirror reflecting our perceived strengths, weaknesses, and overall effectiveness. For example, a leader may feel validated by positive feedback from their team. Still, they may also internalize unspoken signals like disengaged body language during meetings, interpreting these as critiques of their leadership style.

However, as with social comparison, the "mirrors" we rely on aren't always accurate or helpful. We may misinterpret feedback or lean too heavily on external validation to define our self-concept, resulting in misplaced self-doubt or an inflated sense of confidence.

Consider the infamous "American Idol" auditions we can't look away from, where contestants are often emboldened by loved ones who convince them they are talented singers. Though built on faulty mirrors, their self-concept was strong enough to propel them confidently into public performances, sometimes with disastrous results. This humorous yet poignant example reminds us how distorted feedback can inflate or deflate our sense of self.

The looking-glass self shapes leaders long before they step into formal roles. A high-performing individual contributor, for instance, may internalize praise for their technical skills and assume these same strengths naturally translate into effective leadership. A top salesperson might enter a management role, believing their ability to close deals will guarantee success as a leader. While technical expertise is valuable, leadership often demands an entirely different skill set, such as coaching, empathy, and fostering team cohesion.

When leaders rely solely on past feedback or external validation to construct their identity, they risk overestimating their abilities and neglecting areas for growth. Authentic leadership requires bridging the gap between how we've always seen ourselves and the reality of how others experience us in leadership roles. By critically examining these "mirrors" and blending external insights with internal self-awareness, we can develop a self-concept that supports authentic, effective leadership.

REFLECTION QUESTIONS

Whose feedback or opinions have you internalized the most, and how might their perceptions have shaped how you see yourself?

_____

_____

_____

What patterns do you notice in how others respond to your leadership? Are they consistent with how you see yourself?

_____

_____

_____

Family and Early Life Influences

We could explore this factor in great depth and still struggle to do it justice. Simply put, our family upbringing, parental or caregiver expectations, home-life dynamics, and early life experiences significantly shape our self-concept.

Both explicit messages and implicit cues about concepts such as success, responsibility, and self-worth leave lasting impressions that are often difficult to discern because we are too close to them to see them clearly. For example, a leader raised in a family that emphasized independence might develop a self-concept centered on self-reliance, sometimes struggling to ask for help or provide help to their team members. Or someone raised in a collectivist culture might see themselves as a natural team player, sometimes struggling to assert themselves as an individual when it matters most.

While these influences provide a starting point, leaders should evaluate whether these early beliefs still effectively serve them—and their teams—in their current roles.

REFLECTION QUESTIONS

What messages did you hear about success, leadership, or self-worth growing up? How have they shaped your view of yourself today?

_____

_____

_____

How do your early experiences shape your approach to challenges and relationships today?

_____

_____

_____

Cultural and Societal Norms

Cultural and societal norms act as powerful forces in shaping how we see ourselves. They provide implicit and explicit expectations about what it means to be a leader, what success looks like, and how we should behave and communicate in different contexts or roles. These norms are often rooted in the values and traditions of our upbringing and the communities to which we belong.

While they can offer valuable guidance, they can also limit how we define ourselves, especially if we internalize ideals that don't align with our authentic identity. For example, in cultures that prioritize assertiveness and individual achievement, leaders who naturally prefer collaboration and inclusivity may feel pressure to adopt a more competitive style. Similarly, societal norms or narratives about leadership, like the often-touted opinion that strong leaders should never show vulnerability, can discourage leaders from being open about their challenges, even when doing so might build trust and connection with their teams.

In a coaching conversation, one leader shared with me: "Growing up in my culture, I was taught leaders will always have the answers, and that our elders should always have the wisdom we need. But as I've advanced in my career, I've realized that my team doesn't actually expect me to know everything. For them, asking the right questions is often more powerful. I've had to do some un-learning about that to overcome those cultural expectations I place on myself without realizing it." By recognizing the influence of cultural and societal norms, leaders can consciously choose which expectations to embrace and which to question, allowing them to align their leadership approach with their values rather than external pressures.

Cultural and societal norms can constrain us as well as shape us. Racism, sexism, and other forms of discrimination can distort how individuals see themselves and how they're seen by others, often forcing leaders to navigate unfair or limiting expectations. Recognizing these dynamics is part of understanding the full context that shapes our self-concept and resisting the messages that don't align with our values or our worth as people.

REFLECTION QUESTIONS

What cultural or societal norms have shaped your beliefs about yourself?

_____

_____

_____

How do these norms align or conflict with your personal values and leadership style?

_____

_____

_____

What expectations that you've internalized no longer serve you or your team?

_____

_____

_____

Personal Belief Systems and Paradigms

Over time, our personal belief systems become the lenses through which we view ourselves, others, and the world around us. These "paradigms" heavily influence our decisions, behaviors, and the messages we send ourselves about ourselves.

In a recent coaching session, I worked with a leader who described her religious faith as the most important aspect of her identity. She saw her work as a leader as deeply connected to what she believed about God and how God would have her treat others. While walking through a particularly difficult season with her team, where she felt like she was failing, I asked her the following question: "What do you know for certain about yourself?"

She replied quickly, which is significant in my estimation because her answer was grounded in deep convictions:

"When my life or leadership goes off the rails, here's what I know about myself. I am loved by God; there is grace for me, and I'm not defined by my performance, my successes, or my failures."

Her beliefs served as an anchor for her self-concept. While she still had a lot to learn about herself in order to improve her performance, the lens through which she viewed herself was steady and secure. This grounding belief gave her the courage and clarity to lead with resilience, even when giving into self-doubt would have been easier.

Similarly, several years ago, I coached a leader who was a committed Buddhist. When asked a similar question about how he viewed himself, he replied, "In everything I do, I try to see myself as if I'm on a journey to eliminate my pride and ego." For him, this belief provided the foundation for leading with humility.

Our unexamined beliefs may lead to rigid thinking or actions that inadvertently conflict with our broader leadership goals, which is why we should regularly reflect on our beliefs and ensure they align with our evolving values, responsibilities, and the needs of our teams.

Another leader, who didn't identify with any particular faith tradition, had developed a strong personal philosophy shaped by her upbringing and life experiences. She described her core belief as this: "I am here to make things better for people, for systems, and for the spaces I'm in." When I asked her the same question, she said it this way: "No matter what happens, I know I care deeply; I take responsibility, and I will always come back to the work of making things better."

In all three cases, these leaders demonstrated a self-concept rooted in their deepest convictions about the world and our place in it. Their beliefs shaped how they navigated challenges, managed relationships, and prioritized their actions. For each one of us, taking the time to identify and examine these guiding paradigms, religious in nature or otherwise, is essential to refine our self-concept and ensure our actions reflect our most authentic and effective selves.

While these paradigms often provide clarity, motivation, and direction, they can also create blind spots or closed-mindedness about ourselves. Our unexamined beliefs may lead to rigid thinking or actions that inadvertently conflict with our broader leadership goals, which is why we should regularly reflect on our beliefs and ensure they align with our evolving values, responsibilities, and the needs of our teams.

REFLECTION QUESTIONS

What are the personal beliefs or paradigms you hold about yourself that influence your sense of worth, capability, or identity as a leader?

_____

_____

_____

What is one belief you've held about yourself that has consistently guided your decisions or actions as a leader?

_____

_____

_____

Life Events and Transitions

While many of the influences we've discussed up to this point have impacted our self-concept across our lifetimes, we can't forget that our self-concept is sometimes shaped or shaken by significant life events or transitions. Sometimes, sudden promotions, role changes, personal milestones, traumatic events, or unexpected challenges are inflection points that can redefine how we see ourselves. These events, such as a sudden termination or demotion, can be extremely painful.

These moments often force us to confront new realities and question previously held beliefs. For example, stepping into a leadership role for the first time can bring a sense of pride and affirmation about ourselves and the value we bring. Still, a new role can also highlight gaps in skills or confidence that were less apparent to us before. Similarly, a failure or setback might challenge a leader's self-concept, forcing them to reconcile their ideals with their perceived shortcomings. One of my clients shared that she was going through a painful divorce. As a result, she said, "I have struggled to see myself as capable of what I used to think I was capable of before this happened."

While our life events and transitions vary in nature and intensity, they are almost always opportunities for growth, even when they shake the stability of our self-concept. In a recent coaching conversation, a leader reflected on how stepping into a more prominent role reshaped her self-understanding: "I always thought I was a great team player, but leading this group made me realize I've always relied on collaboration to avoid making tough decisions on my own."

Major life events and transitions often act as pivotal moments in our leadership journey, offering valuable opportunities to assess our strengths and confront areas of vulnerability.

These experiences remind us that leadership isn't static; it's a fluid and evolving process shaped by the roles we step into and the challenges we navigate along the way.

REFLECTION QUESTIONS

What significant events or transitions have shaped your self-concept?

_____

_____

_____

How has a new role or challenge highlighted strengths or exposed areas for growth in your leadership?

_____

_____

_____

What lessons have you learned about yourself during moments of significant change?

_____

_____

_____

Your Ideal Self

One final influence I want to highlight is one we often take for granted—our *ideal self*, which significantly impacts our self-concept. Our ideal self represents the version of ourselves we aspire to be: the qualities, behaviors, and values we hope to embody. Psychologist Carl Rogers described it as a vision of our best possible self, shaped by our personal ambitions, cultural ideals, and the expectations of those around us.[19] For leaders, this ideal self often acts as both a motivator and a benchmark, driving growth while also highlighting the gaps between where they are now and where they want to be.

This gap between the current self and the ideal self can feel like a double-edged sword. On the one hand, it inspires us to improve, pushing us toward intentional growth. On the other, it can create frustration or even feelings of inadequacy when our current abilities or actions don't align with our aspirations. For example, a leader who sees their ideal self as calm and composed under pressure might feel disheartened when they react emotionally in stressful situations. However, it's important to recognize that this tension is a natural part of the growth process. Rather than seeing the gap as a failure, it can be reframed as a signpost for progress.

This might sound something like:

"I've always seen myself as someone who seeks to empower others. Lately, I've realized how often I step in and take over instead of empowering others to do the work. My ideal self is someone who leads with trust and lets my team shine, but I know I'm not there yet."

When we use our ideal selves in healthy ways to challenge ourselves to grow, the honest acknowledgment of the gap between our current and ideal selves can become a powerful catalyst for our success. The key is to approach this gap with curiosity rather than self-judgment. Our ideal self should act as a compass, guiding our decisions and behaviors—and not as a source of self-criticism. It's a vision to strive toward, not a standard to be perfectly achieved overnight.

REFLECTION QUESTIONS

How would you describe your ideal self?

___

___

___

In what ways does your current leadership align with this vision? Where does it differ?

___

___

___

How can you reframe the gap between your current and ideal self as an opportunity for growth rather than a limitation?

___

___

___

From Insight to Impact: The Seven Pillars of Congruent Leadership

By now, you've spent some time reflecting on how your self-concept has been shaped by your experiences, values, upbringing, and cultural context. Maybe you paused to consider the Reflection Questions. Maybe you zoomed past them (no shame!). Either way, this kind of reflection is important. The more clearly we understand how we've come to see ourselves, the more intentionally we can show up as leaders.

But self-awareness alone doesn't change behavior. And clarity without action won't build trust. That's why I developed the *Seven Pillars of Congruent Leadership* as a practical framework drawn from my work with coaching clients, teams, and leaders across industries and shaped by my background in communication and psychology. To help you visualize the journey, imagine a strong, well-built structure. At the foundation is your self-concept—your understanding of who you are, shaped by your values, beliefs, and lived experiences. Rising from this foundation are seven interconnected pillars, each representing a key focus area for the kind of growth we're aiming for. Together they form the framework of congruent leadership—the powerful alignment between how you see yourself and how others experience you.

The framework begins with mindset, then moves into personal alignment, strengths-based leadership, limitations, perception, other-awareness, and ultimately your leadership impact and legacy. These are the habits and insights I've seen transform frustrated, overwhelmed, or out-of-sync leaders into ones who are grounded, trusted, and effective.

The good news? You don't need to master every pillar in chronological order before moving on to the next. They're not a checklist, which is surprising coming from me, for I am

SELF-CONCEPT

nothing if not a checklist gal. The pillars are interconnected practices that support and reinforce one another, helping you build a leadership presence rooted in clarity, consistency, and credibility. They invite you to lean into your strengths, examine your limitations and blind spots, and approach feedback with courage and curiosity. This deeply personal process helps you understand yourself at your core. Congruent leadership begins with internal alignment, but it comes alive in relationships—shaping the trust you build and the transformation you inspire in others.

As you develop clarity in each area, from pursuing self-awareness with courage to owning your legacy, you create alignment between your internal identity and your external leadership. This framework serves as both a mirror and a map: it helps you see yourself more clearly and chart a course toward greater integrity, trust, and influence.

In the chapters ahead, we'll explore each of these pillars, moving from mindset to outward impact. You'll learn how to cultivate leadership that's more effective and more deeply rooted in who you truly are.

Here's a sneak peek:

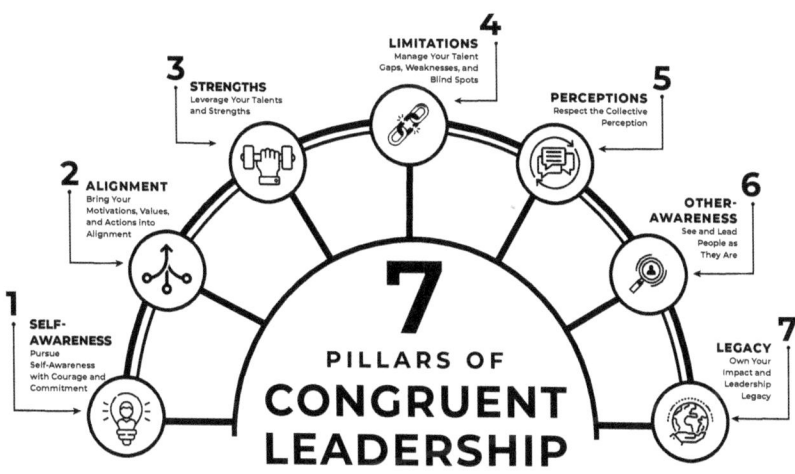

PILLAR ONE:

Pursue Self-Awareness with Courage and Commitment

Self-awareness sounds nice in theory, but in practice, it requires grit. Pillar One is about adopting a growth mindset and staying curious (even when it's uncomfortable). Courage and commitment are the mindset fuel that drive personal transformation.

PILLAR TWO:

Bring Your Motivations, Values, and Actions into Alignment

There's nothing more frustrating than a leader who says one thing and does another. This pillar helps you identify your core motivations and values and then make sure your leadership behaviors are in sync with them.

PILLAR THREE:
Leverage Your Talents and Strengths

Your natural strengths are your leadership superpowers. However, too often, leaders overlook what makes them uniquely effective. Pillar Three is about knowing what you bring to the table, investing in it, and using it intentionally to drive results and build trust.

PILLAR FOUR:
Manage Your Talent Gaps, Weaknesses, and Blind Spots

We all have limitations and are aware of some and not others. This pillar is about getting honest with what you tend to overuse, avoid, or deny, and learning to manage those gaps through awareness, support, and humility.

PILLAR FIVE:
Respect the Collective Perception

This pillar challenges you to consider how others experience your leadership. That means listening, interpreting feedback wisely, and aligning your intentions with your impact. Trust and credibility grow when you take others' perceptions seriously.

PILLAR SIX:
See and Lead People as They Are

Great leadership isn't just about knowing yourself—it's about deeply knowing others. This pillar focuses on curiosity, empathy, and the power of seeing people as individuals.

PILLAR SEVEN:

Own Your Impact and Leadership Legacy

Every choice you make shapes the experience of those around you, and over time, those choices define the culture, values, and outcomes you leave behind. This pillar invites you to lead with the future in mind, to influence with intention, and to build a legacy rooted in clarity, trust, and purpose.

Now, let's take the first step. You don't have to have it all figured out. You just need the willingness to grow. Let's make it happen.

PILLAR ONE

SELF-AWARENESS

CHAPTER 3

Pursue Self-Awareness with Courage and Commitment

Key Question: *How can you pursue self-awareness by balancing confidence in your leadership with the curiosity needed to grow and improve?*

IT'S NOT EASY TO admit when your leadership isn't working. Most of us don't set out to create dysfunction, and it can be painful to realize that our best efforts, or even our blind spots, have created an environment where trust is low and morale is even lower. But for leaders committed to growth, that moment of realization can become a powerful turning point.

Years ago, during an initial coaching session, one of my new clients, a senior executive known for his entrepreneurial drive and industry accomplishments, took a deep breath and said, "Something obviously isn't working, and I think I'm past the point of being able to fix this on my own. I need help, which is really hard to admit to myself, let alone everyone I work with."

Though his leadership had long been described as "intense," the situation had escalated. His team wasn't just disengaged—they were actively withdrawing and pushing back against his leadership. His unpredictable moods, emotional reactivity, and patronizing communication style had created an environment defined by fear and control. The damage was real, and it was clear that change couldn't wait.

These first conversations with a client are tricky to navigate. Fortunately, this client brought a healthy amount of humility to the table. While getting to know him and discussing our coaching goals, which felt quite urgent to all involved, I asked him what barriers might prevent us from reaching said goals.

He paused for about twenty seconds, which felt like an eternity, mind you. He then leaned into the Zoom frame even more, and said, "I'm scared."

"I'm scared that I've ruined my reputation and that I'll never gain their respect back."

"When have you done scary things before and achieved great outcomes?" I asked him.

He began to list past experiences in which he had done something brave despite feeling threatened and vulnerable.

"What makes this scary thing different from those experiences?"

"This makes me confront parts of myself that I'm uncomfortable coming face-to-face with," he replied.

"Based on this feedback you've received, how often do you think your team members come face-to-face with that part of you?"

He looked up and said, as if he realized the weightiness of it for the first time, "Every damn day."

Over the next several months, he did the courageous work of digging into the unproductive leadership and communication patterns that got him and his team in this position. He committed to listening intently, resisting defensiveness, and slowly rebuilding trust. Restoration didn't happen overnight, to be sure, but brick by brick, he laid a new foundation he could build upon. His learning posture afforded him so much throughout the coaching journey. I think of him often when teaching and training on Pillar One, which is all about pursuing personal growth with courage and commitment. Because growth and development require both.

Seeing ourselves through the lens of others' experiences takes courage—the kind of courage that gives us an honest perspective about how our leadership is received and how our behavior impacts those around us. Growth demands that we confront hard truths, recognize both our strengths and our blind spots, and take deliberate steps to change what isn't working.

Personal growth also requires sustained commitment. When self-reflection feels uncomfortable, commitment keeps us engaged, reminding us that discomfort is temporary, but the transformation is lasting. Self-awareness is not a single moment of clarity; it's an ongoing process of learning, unlearning, and refining how we lead.

Think of the leaders that you respect the most. In addition to all the tactical things they do well, like communicating clearly, advocating for you, or caring for you as an individual, they also likely bring a healthy mindset to their leadership rhythms. As a follower, you likely benefit from their mindset on a daily basis.

That's because effective leadership requires us to "get our minds right." Before we ever say a word or make a decision as leaders, our mindset—how we interpret situations and frame other people's actions—shapes everything we do. It influences how we communicate, make sense of feedback, handle setbacks, and even view ourselves in relation to our teams.

If we want to lead congruently by aligning our values, actions, and impact, we must come to the table with a mindset open to learning and growth. No leader reaches their full potential without the willingness to evolve, challenge assumptions, and refine their approach based on experience and feedback.

Growth is often painful, and our tendency is often to avoid it at all costs, especially when it comes at the expense of our self-concept. It would have been very easy for my client to react defensively and dig his heels in, blaming others for the outcomes he was getting with his team. But he came to the conclusion that it was better to grow through the pain than continue with the methods that weren't serving his team members or the organization well.

His mindset was everything. His willingness to face discomfort was the first step in shifting his mindset, moving from certainty about who he thought he was as a leader to curiosity about who he could become.

Entire books have been written on the importance of leadership mindset. While I won't do it full justice here, let me show you two frameworks that have helped my clients (and me) grow with courage.

Fixed Versus Growth Mindset: Are You Clinging to Certainty or Committed to Growth?

Psychologist Carol Dweck's research on fixed and growth mindsets provides a framework for understanding how we tend to engage with challenges and learning opportunities.[20]

A *fixed mindset* says: "This is just who I am." Leaders with a fixed mindset likely see their abilities and tendencies as static. They may avoid feedback, feel threatened by others' success, or resist change. They are less likely to seek out learning opportunities because they feel certain of who they are.

A *growth mindset* says: "I can improve and evolve." These leaders view challenges as opportunities to stretch themselves and discover what they're capable of. They actively seek feedback, embrace the awkward and uncomfortable as part of learning, and recognize that skills, including leadership, are developed over time, not predetermined by our personalities, existing skills, or abilities.

If we apply this framework specifically to self-awareness:

A fixed mindset leader might hear critical feedback and think, *This is just how I lead—if they don't like it, that's their problem.*

But a growth mindset leader hears feedback and asks, *What can I learn from this, and how can I adapt to be more effective?*

Sometimes when I'm facilitating leadership development programs, someone will say something like, "You can't teach an old dog new tricks" or "I've been through every leadership development program in the book, and I've heard it all."

When I hear leaders share sentiments like that, my first thought is, *I wonder how that fixed mindset is negatively impacting them and the outcomes they get.*

Performance Versus Learning Mindset: Are You Trying to Prove or Improve?

Beyond fixed versus growth mindsets, another helpful distinction is whether a leader operates from a performance mindset or a learning mindset. Dweck, along with Ellen Leggett, introduced this concept through their work on achievement motivation.[21] They found that people tend to pursue goals either to demonstrate their competence (performance orientation) or to develop it (learning orientation).

Leaders with a *performance mindset* are primarily focused

on proving their competence. Every decision, presentation, or feedback conversation feels like a test of their abilities. When things go poorly, they feel it defines their leadership. They're often hard on themselves, cycling through shame and fear when things don't go as planned or when outcomes don't meet expectations.

By contrast, leaders with a *learning mindset* prioritize growth over image. They view mistakes as necessary for progress and value feedback as a tool for development. They're less likely to crumble under pressure or hide their missteps because the focus is on learning and not looking perfect. Instead of fearing being wrong, they focus on what they can take away from the experience. They don't feel as threatened if other people see them struggle or fail.

Here's a simple check-in to see what you might default to when it comes to your mindset:

When you think back to a recent leadership challenge, did your first thought sound like:

- *I should have done better—I need to prove I belong here* (performance mindset), or

- *That didn't go as I hoped—what can I learn from this for next time* (learning mindset)?

If you're discovering that you tend toward a fixed or performance mindset, you're in good company. I often tell leaders in my workshops that I still drift toward that thinking myself. I've always been very hard on myself and spent too much energy comparing myself to others. What I have learned over the years, and will likely always need to continue preaching to myself, is that personal growth requires risks, some failure sprinkled in, and some misses. A growth and learning mindset keeps me centered on what matters most in leadership, which are the people who deserve my best mindset.

The way we frame challenges, feedback, and setbacks determines our capacity for leadership growth. Shifting from a fixed or performance mindset to a growth and learning mindset frees us to take risks, seek honest feedback, and embrace the process of growth without fear of failure. I've learned that I lead best when I stop trying to prove something and start focusing on learning. What about you?

The Confidence and Curiosity Balance

Our mindsets set the pace for us in many ways, and great leaders walk a fine line between confidence in themselves and curiosity about how they are experienced by others. They trust their experience and instincts while remaining open to learning. This balance enables them to grow without becoming overly self-critical or, conversely, so self-assured that they fail to recognize their blind spots.

Too much confidence without curiosity can lead to stagnation and un-self-aware leadership. When leaders assume they already have the answers, they stop seeking new perspectives. They dismiss feedback, believing that if something has worked in the past, it will always work. This mindset can create an environment where others hesitate to speak up, fearing their input won't be valued. Worse, it can leave leaders blind to shifts in their teams or industries, making them out of touch.

On the other hand, too much curiosity without confidence can be just as damaging. Leaders who constantly second-guess themselves often struggle to make decisions. They may rely too heavily on outside opinions, place their identity in others' opinions, and be afraid to trust their instincts. Their teams sense the uncertainty, leading to confusion and a lack of direction. When leaders constantly question themselves, their credibility erodes, and their teams feel unstable.

I can't count the number of times I've heard a leader in a team workshop say something like, "We're a family around here" or "I see myself as a servant leader," only to see team members dart their eyes at one another or text under the table as if to say, "Can you believe they just said that?" This is a classic example of a confidence-over-curiosity imbalance. The leader is certain about how they see themselves, but they haven't remained curious about how others actually experience them.

Conversely, I've seen leaders struggle with the opposite problem—apologizing too much, over-explaining, or getting stuck in imposter syndrome. They worry excessively about how they're perceived, questioning every decision and eroding their leadership presence in the process. Their uncertainty makes their teams uneasy as people look to leaders for clarity and direction.

Healthy leaders balance both confidence and curiosity. They trust in their abilities but remain open to learning and feedback. This isn't about constantly second-guessing yourself in a way that breeds self-doubt. It's about staying engaged with how your leadership is perceived and ensuring your actions align with your impact.

Moreover, great leaders don't just assume they're getting it right. They check in. They ask. They adjust. A confident yet curious leader listens as much as they speak. They welcome feedback as a tool for refinement and don't consider it a challenge to their authority. They ask, "How did that land with you?" or "What am I missing?" from a desire to lead with clarity and awareness.

This is why I get a little nervous when I see leadership content that promotes the idea of "Who cares what people think of you?" Seriously, the last time I went to a bookstore to review the titles of new leadership books, I was struck by how many seem to be sending the message that other people's opinions about us aren't important. While it's true that leaders shouldn't be controlled by external opinions, it's dangerous to dismiss them altogether. Self-awareness isn't about disregarding how others experience us; it's about ensuring our leadership presence aligns with our intentions.

Confidence and curiosity create a powerful leadership presence when they work together. Confidence allows us to act decisively, to set a vision, and move forward with conviction. Curiosity keeps us adaptable, ensuring we remain open to new insights and willing to adjust our course when necessary.

To become the kind of leaders our teams need, we must embrace personal growth with courage and commitment. Confidence or curiosity alone won't get us there. But together, they create a leadership style rooted in strength, adaptability, and a willingness to grow.

We can assess our confidence and curiosity balance by asking ourselves questions like:

- Do I seek feedback regularly, or do I assume I already know how I'm perceived?

- Am I paranoid about what others think of me to the point it undermines my credibility?

- Do I hesitate to make decisions out of fear of getting it wrong?

- When was the last time I adjusted my leadership approach based on input from others?

Locus of Control: Who's in Charge of Your Growth?

Let's look at our mindsets from another angle that has been helpful for many of my clients. Our mindsets are heavily influenced by what psychologists call *locus of control*—the degree to which we believe we have control over our circumstances and outcomes. Psychologist Julian Rotter, who introduced the concept of locus of control, suggested that individuals tend to view the outcomes in their lives as either a result of their own actions (internal locus) or shaped by external forces beyond their control (external locus).[22]

Leaders with an *external locus of control* believe that their success or failure is dictated by outside forces like luck, difficult team members, bad leadership above them, or circumstances beyond their control. This mindset often leads to blame, frustration, and a sense of powerlessness.

Leaders with an *internal locus of control* believe that their growth and effectiveness come from their choices, habits, and ability to adapt. They take ownership of their learning, seek resources, and work to improve their leadership.

Consider the difference: A leader with an external locus of control might blame "bad hires" for team dysfunction, while a leader with an internal locus would ask, "How can I better set expectations and coach my team?"

Leaders with an internal locus of control often experience greater emotional stability and a stronger sense of agency,[23] because they believe their actions can influence outcomes, which drives accountability and growth. However, it's important to recognize that an external locus of control isn't always negative. In situations that are truly beyond a leader's control, such as market shifts, economic downturns, or unforeseen organizational changes, external attribution can help maintain perspective, reduce unnecessary self-blame, and protect confidence during stressful periods.

Shifting Toward an Internal Locus of Control

One of the most powerful mindset shifts a leader can make is replacing deflection and blame with ownership. This begins with a simple, courageous question:

"What is one leadership challenge I've been blaming on external factors, and what is one concrete action I can take to influence a better outcome?"

This isn't about denying the realities outside your control. It's about reclaiming the space where your choices do matter. Rather than seeing yourself as a passive participant in your leadership environment, consider the choices you can make that meaningfully shape your outcomes and influence your team.

Instead of: "I can't build a great team because our hiring process is broken."

Try this: "I may not control every hiring decision, but I can set clearer expectations, improve onboarding, and invest in developing the people I do have."

The most congruent leaders own their growth. They recognize that while they can't control everything, they can control how they respond, seek feedback, and develop their skills. This small but powerful mindset shift helps leaders move from feeling stuck to taking meaningful action, building a sense of agency, and strengthening their leadership presence.

Where Do You Place Control?

Take a few minutes to reflect on your natural tendencies when things go wrong, or when things go right.

1. When faced with a leadership challenge, do you tend to focus more on external circumstances or your own response?
    - What kinds of things do you typically blame or credit?
    - Do certain situations push you more toward an external or internal locus?

2. Think about a recent situation where something didn't go as planned.
    - How did you explain what happened to yourself or others?
    - If you leaned toward external attribution, what part of that situation could you influence going forward?

3. What's one area of your leadership where you want to take greater ownership?
    - What would shifting your mindset in that area look like?

Six Growth Practices to Develop Self-Awareness

Below are six powerful practices to help you grow in self-awareness. Over the years I've done this work, these practices have helped leaders see themselves more clearly, lead more congruently, and grow with purpose. Each of these will show up again throughout the rest of the book. For now, notice which ones feel familiar and which ones stretch you a bit.

1. **Reflective Practices.** This includes journaling, note-taking, or simply carving out intentional time to think about how you're showing up. It's how you spot patterns in your thoughts and behaviors and begin to connect the dots between what you value and how you lead.

2. **Mindfulness and Self-Monitoring.** Mindfulness isn't just for yoga mats. Leaders who pay attention to what they're thinking, feeling, and doing in real time are better equipped to adjust their behavior. Self-monitoring is like an internal leadership radar and helps you recognize when you're aligned and when you're not.

3. **Observation and Behavior Analysis.** This one's about studying yourself like you study your team. Are there recurring communication breakdowns? Emotional triggers? Moments when you lead with strength or step into stress? Observing your behavior gives you data you can act on.

4. **Coaching and Mentorship.** Sometimes you need an outside voice to help you hear the inside noise. Coaches and mentors can reflect back what you might miss, challenge your assumptions, and help you grow with accountability and support.

5. **Practicing Self-Disclosure.** Letting yourself be known

is a growth practice. When you share your struggles, goals, or leadership journey with trusted others, you create space for connection, feedback, and trust.

6. **Seeking Feedback.** Self-aware leaders invite feedback. They ask others how they're doing informally and frequently and not only during formal reviews. They know that blind spots don't disappear on their own. Those spots grow smaller when we shine a light on them.

We'll explore each of these more deeply in later chapters, but these are the tools that build congruence over time. The more consistently you use them, the more clearly you'll see yourself. And the more effectively you'll lead others.

Quirky but Practical Ways to Grow in Self-Awareness

Because soul-searching doesn't always have to be so serious. Ready to get a little weird? Here are some off-the-beaten-path ways to explore how you're wired, how others might see you, and what's going on under the hood of your leadership. Not all will work for everyone—but hey, self-awareness loves experimentation.

1. Ask Your Favorite AI Agent

- ☐ "What kind of leader do you think I am based on this email/text/slack message?"

- ☐ "What's something you know about me that I might not realize about myself?"

- ☐ "What's a blind spot someone with my strengths might have?"

- ☐ "Based on the questions I've asked you recently, what should I know about my mindset?"

Yes, it's a little meta—asking AI to help you understand yourself. Yes, it works. Your AI sidekick won't judge you and might surprise you.

2. Google Yourself (While Pretending You're a Stranger)

Open an incognito browser tab, google yourself, and try to interpret your digital footprint like you've never met you. What's the vibe? What's missing? Is the version of you online someone you'd trust to lead a team?

3. Analyze Your Fitness Tracker Data

Seriously—look at your recovery trends or sleep patterns after emotionally tough workdays. Are there clues about how your body responds to stress, conflict, or big wins? If your heart rate spikes every time you check Slack, maybe that tells you something.

4. Ask a Barista (or Bartender or Hair Stylist): "What's Your First Impression of Me?"
Disclaimer: Only do this if you're okay hearing the truth. People who encounter you without context can offer shockingly accurate vibes-based feedback. You don't need a deep dive, just a casual "What's something you noticed about me right away?"

What We're Not Going to Do

Before we go any further, let's be clear about what this journey isn't. This book isn't an invitation to wallow in shame, spiral into self-loathing, overanalyze yourself, or over-identify with your flaws. And it certainly isn't another tool for self-criticism disguised as self-awareness. This is the kind of thing that has kept me up at night about writing this book. I want to help leaders see themselves clearly. I do not want to cause harm.

Dr. Eurich, previously mentioned in chapter one, has studied thousands of leaders on the topic of self-awareness, and her research reveals a surprising truth: Not all introspection is helpful.[24] In fact, asking the wrong questions, especially the self-critical kind, can actually make us less self-aware. Eurich calls this the "introspection trap," where leaders get stuck in endless loops of asking "Why am I like this?" without gaining clarity or making progress. Instead, she suggests better questions like, "What am I noticing?" or "What's one thing I can do differently?" These questions move us toward insight and action, rather than shame and paralysis.

That's the posture I want to invite you into: one that's

grounded in curiosity and not judgment. We grow not by tearing ourselves apart but by understanding ourselves with honesty and grace. Self-awareness isn't about overthinking everything or constantly second-guessing yourself. It's about creating just enough space to examine how your beliefs, behaviors, and patterns are serving you and how they're not. From there, you get to decide what kind of leader you want to be.

Shame is not a leadership strategy. If you've internalized the idea that being hard on yourself is the only way to be accountable, I want to challenge that. Shame doesn't create stronger leaders. It creates leaders who hide and disconnect and shrink back in defensiveness. We grow by understanding ourselves and not by judging ourselves.

While this book will challenge you, it will never shame you. The seven pillars ask you to take full responsibility for your growth without self-blame.

One of the reminders I come back to often, especially when I'm being hard on myself, is from researcher and storyteller Brené Brown, whose work on vulnerability and self-compassion has shaped how so many of us think about courage. She writes, "Talk to yourself the way you'd talk to someone you love."[25] For many high-achieving leaders, that's the hardest part, isn't it?

It's easy to extend grace to others and withhold it from ourselves. But if we want to grow in meaningful, sustainable ways, we have to treat ourselves with the same compassion and dignity we offer the people we lead.

So no, we're not going to become self-aware by beating ourselves up. We're going to become self-aware by getting honest, staying open, and walking forward with compassion.

That's why this journey calls for:

- Courage to face what's true.

- Commitment to keep going.

- Curiosity to explore without judgment.

- Confidence to believe we're capable of change.

- And yes—Compassion to hold yourself gently in the process.

(And no, I didn't set out to collect a bunch of "C-words," but I think we're in too deep to stop now.)

As we move on, let's remember this: Pursuing self-awareness with courage and commitment transforms us *and* strengthens the experience of everyone we lead.

That's the real work of personal growth: closing the gap between our good intentions and the outcomes we're actually creating. Pillar One has helped us start that process of learning how to get honest with ourselves, stay open, and shift our mindsets so we can lead from a place of responsibility rather than reactivity. But now it's time to go a step deeper.

In the next chapter, we'll explore Pillar Two, and how to bring your values, motivations, and actions into alignment, because congruence isn't just about knowing yourself. It's about leading in a way that's consistent with what matters most.

PILLAR TWO

ALIGNMENT

CHAPTER 4

Bring Your Motivations, Values, and Actions into Alignment

Key Question: *In what ways are your actions aligned, or misaligned, with your core values and motivations?*

A LEADER I COACHED (we'll call him Josiah) once told me, "I've always told my teams that I value collaboration in decision-making, but my 360 review says they don't see me that way at all. That really hurts to hear, but if I'm honest with myself, they're right. I make decisions alone more often than I should."

These "aha" moments, as uncomfortable as they may be, are opportunities to acknowledge the gap between what we claim to value and how we actually show up. This is the essence of leadership congruence. When our motivations, values, and actions align, we build trust, consistency, and credibility with our team members. But when they don't, we create ambiguity, disengagement, and even resentment.

We would all likely agree that leadership is more than what we *intend*—it's about the *impact* we have and what we demonstrate through our daily decisions and interactions.

But it's all too common that we fail to see the areas in our leadership where misalignment has crept in. If we were flies on the wall in our organizations' hallways, on Zoom calls, or text threads between our team members, we might hear the specific areas where they find us inauthentic or out of touch.

While that's an uncomfortable thought, to be sure, it's an important thought exercise to consider the areas where we are not in harmony with what we say is important to us. This chapter's ultimate goal is to help us bridge the gap between what we say we value and what our actions communicate to others.

We'll unpack our core motivations, explore the values we claim, and examine how all of that translates into daily leadership behaviors. Because when our motivations, values, and actions are in sync, our leadership becomes more trusted, consistent, and effective.

Motivations: What's Driving Your Leadership?

Our motivations to lead others shape how we lead. Some of us were drawn to leadership because we wanted to make an impact on the world, develop and mentor others, or build something meaningful in our organization. Others stepped into leadership out of necessity or opportunity, learning as they went, and with various levels of enthusiasm about the process.

No shame if this sounds like you! I've worked with so many leaders who say, "I never thought I would be a manager, but here I am anyway," or "I actually prefer to work autonomously, but in my organization, if you don't manage others, you can't get promoted." Regardless of how we got here, our motivations and values influence and guide us, shaping how we engage with our teams and the team culture we build.

Motivations influence why we lead and impact *how* we lead. They shape our strengths, blind spots, and interaction with others. Consider a leader primarily motivated by competence—someone who deeply values being knowledgeable, capable, and prepared. This motivation can lead to strengths like thorough planning, excellence in execution, and a strong sense of responsibility. But when overemphasized, it can also create hesitation to delegate, reluctance to take risks, or a tendency to overanalyze and delay action until things feel "perfect."

(Have you read enough to discern this one hits home with me?)

Let's look at one more. What about the leader primarily motivated by approval—someone who places a high value on being liked, respected, or validated by others? This motivation can foster strong relationships, empathy, and diplomacy. But if left unchecked, it can also lead to conflict avoidance, inconsistent decision-making, or prioritizing popularity over accountability.

To be sure, none of these motivations are inherently flawed. The key is recognizing what drives you, where it serves you well, and where it might hold you back. That's the heart of self-awareness. By understanding your core motivations, you can make intentional adjustments to ensure they support, rather than hinder, your leadership effectiveness.

Intrinsic Versus Extrinsic Motivation

According to motivation researchers Edward Deci and Richard Ryan, intrinsic motivation and extrinsic motivation are two distinct forces that shape human behavior and goal pursuit.[26]

Intrinsic motivation is driven by internal fulfillment—the sense of purpose, meaning, or personal growth that leadership provides. A leader motivated by service may find deep satisfaction in mentoring and empowering others. Someone motivated by learning may thrive in leadership because it offers continual opportunities to expand their knowledge and expertise.

Extrinsic motivation is driven by external rewards, such as compensation, status, reputation, or recognition. There's nothing wrong with these motivators; they can be powerful incentives. A leader motivated by achievement might thrive on hitting ambitious goals. Someone who values security might view leadership as a way to maintain stability in their career.

The key is recognizing how your dominant motivations shape your leadership. Are they leading you toward behaviors that build trust, engage your team, and drive positive outcomes? Or are they causing you to default to patterns that don't serve your long-term success?

When I work with leaders one-on-one, I often ask them to identify and confront their intrinsic and extrinsic motivations. While both are powerful, it is essential to find at least a few intrinsic motivators during seasons when our extrinsic motivators are failing.

These examples show how intrinsic and extrinsic motivation play out in leadership and why intrinsic motivators are essential when external rewards fall short:

The High-Achieving Leader Who Loses a Promotion

A leader who is primarily driven by external recognition and career advancement (extrinsic motivation) might struggle if they are passed over for a promotion. They may feel unfulfilled or resentful without a strong intrinsic motivator, such as a passion for developing others or solving meaningful problems. However, if they are also driven by a deep desire to mentor and grow their team, they can find purpose in their work even when the title and external validation are absent.

The Sales Manager in a Tough Economy

A leader in a sales-driven role may thrive on hitting revenue targets and earning performance-based bonuses. But in a downturn, when those extrinsic rewards are scarce, their motivation could plummet. If they have an intrinsic motivator, like a love of building relationships or the challenge of problem-solving, they are more likely to stay engaged and resilient, even in challenging times.

The Leader Who Loves Public Praise but Faces Tough Feedback

A leader who thrives on external validation and being seen as competent might be deeply discouraged when they receive critical/evaluative feedback or aren't publicly recognized for their work. But suppose they also have a strong intrinsic motivator, such as a commitment to continuous learning or personal growth. In that case, they can reframe criticism as an opportunity to improve rather than a threat to their identity.

Extrinsic motivators like money, promotions, and awards are important, but they are unpredictable and often temporary. Intrinsic motivators like personal growth, a commitment to others, and a sense of purpose help sustain us when external rewards are lacking. Effective leaders cultivate both, ensuring they have an internal source of motivation that keeps them engaged even when circumstances are challenging.

What If I Don't Even Want to Be a Leader?

Some of you might be reading this and thinking, *I didn't ask for this. I don't even want to lead other people!* That's an important point to consider. Some people step into leadership with a clear sense of purpose and excitement. Others find themselves in leadership because they were promoted for their individual performance, handed a team without much say, or given responsibility because no one else was ready or able to step up to the plate.

If that's where you find yourself, here's the most important thing to know: Leadership isn't about having a title or a desire to be in charge. Interestingly, research out of Harvard found that people who strongly prefer to be in charge often underperform compared to those who are randomly assigned to leadership roles.[27] The researchers suggest that those most eager to lead may overestimate their abilities or underestimate the relational and emotional skills effective leadership requires. In other words, wanting the title doesn't necessarily mean you're ready for the role. This reminds us that motivation matters, not just in getting the job, but in how we show up for it.

So, whether you want the role or not, people are looking to you for direction, support, and clarity. The question isn't, "Do I want to be a leader?" but "How do I want to lead now that other people depend on me to support and empower them?"

Rather than focusing on whether leadership is your long-term path, consider the impact you want to have while in this role. What kind of leader do you wish you had? How can you make leadership a meaningful experience, even if it's not your favorite or forever role?

Even if you don't see yourself leading for the rest of your career, how you show up now can shape your team's success, career trajectory, and sense of purpose and fulfillment. By clarifying your motivations, aligning them with your values, and choosing to lead with intention, you can create a leadership presence that is both authentic and impactful, whether you chose this path or not.

To lead with impact, we need motivation that fuels the leadership behaviors that create great outcomes. If our motivation is unclear or misaligned, we may default to behaviors that feel natural but don't necessarily serve our people or our goals.

Take a moment to reflect on what truly drives you as a leader.

REFLECTION QUESTIONS

Why did I step into leadership? What originally drew me to this role?

___

___

___

What energizes me most about leading? When do I feel most fulfilled?

___

___

___

What frustrates me most about leadership? Does my frustration reveal anything about my deeper motivations?

_____

_____

_____

How do I measure my success as a leader? Is it based on team performance, personal achievement, external validation, or alignment with my values?

_____

_____

_____

What do I think my team members would say about what motivates me?

_____

_____

_____

What kind of impact do I want to have while I'm in this role, and what would it look like to lead with purpose and not just obligation?

_____

_____

_____

Values: What Do You Stand For?

Beyond our motivations, we all lead from a set of beliefs and core values. Some we've named clearly, and others we've never put into words. These values are shaped by our experiences, personalities, cultures, and even the leaders who influenced us early in our careers. Whether we realize it or not, they shape how we set priorities, how we respond to pressure, and how we show up for the people who count on us.

But here's the catch: Just because we say we value something doesn't mean we actually live it.

Suppose a leader fundamentally believes that people should be self-sufficient and shouldn't need much affirmation. In that case, they may minimize the importance of recognition in the workplace, insisting that employees should be motivated simply by "doing their job." In turn, they may fail to acknowledge or celebrate achievements, leading to increased disengagement and frustration among their team members. This isn't because they don't care but because their value system doesn't emphasize recognition as a leadership priority.

A leader, like my coaching client who claimed to value collaboration but consistently made unilateral decisions, may not have an intentionally defined value system. They may see themselves as collaborative because they believe in teamwork at a conceptual level, but their actions don't align with the reality of how they engage with others.

That disconnect happens to all of us. Maybe we say we value developing others, but we're constantly too busy to coach, delegate, or check in with our team in a meaningful way. Maybe we pride ourselves on fairness, but we tend to show more grace to people who think like us. Or maybe we think of ourselves as humble, but we bristle every time feedback comes our way.

This means we're human—not hypocrites. And if we're serious about congruence, we have to be willing to look at the difference between our *aspirational values* (the things we *want* to believe we prioritize) and our *actual values* (the things we *truly* prioritize, as evidenced by our behavior).

It's uncomfortable to sort that out. As leaders, we're moving fast, reacting to pressure, making decisions in the moment. But if we don't pause to get clear on what we stand for, and what we want to stand for, we risk making decisions based on urgency, fear, or outside expectations instead of what truly matters.

Consider this example:

A leader believes they value work-life balance and tells their team they encourage boundaries. But if that same leader routinely works late, answers emails on weekends, and expects immediate responses at all hours, their *real* value is something different, perhaps achievement or responsiveness. Their words say one thing, but their actions reflect another.

That's why value clarity matters. When we know what we truly stand for, we lead more intentionally. We make decisions that reflect our beliefs.

But it's one thing to say you value something. It's another to live it consistently. The people you lead are always paying attention to whether your behavior backs up your beliefs, especially when the pressure's on. Below are some common leadership values, along with examples of what they might look like in action and what it looks like when they're missing. This list of values isn't exhaustive, so think outside the box or table to determine the values that hold meaning for you.

Value	Aligned Behavior	Misaligned Behavior
INTEGRITY	Follows through on commitments	Avoids accountability
	Communicates honestly, even when it's difficult	Spins or omits the truth
	Admits mistakes and takes responsibility	Makes exceptions for themselves
HUMILITY	Owns mistakes	Gets defensive when challenged
	Asks for input from others	Needs to be seen as the smartest person in the room
	Gives credit and praise freely	Takes credit for team efforts
RELATIONSHIPS	Invests time in building trust and rapport	Skips check-ins or cancels 1:1s regularly
	Follows up personally and professionally	Focuses only on performance or results
	Prioritizes people, not just tasks, in daily interactions	Ignores relational tension or unspoken team dynamics

Value	Aligned Behavior	Misaligned Behavior
ACCOUNTABILITY	Sets clear expectations	Avoids difficult conversations
	Follows through consistently	Makes vague promises
	Addresses missed commitments directly	Inconsistently holds others (or themselves) responsible
EMPATHY	Listens to understand, not just to respond	Dismisses emotional cues or concerns
	Checks in on team members' well-being	Assumes intent without asking
	Adapts to individual needs when appropriate	Pushes performance over people
COLLABORATION	Seeks diverse input before deciding	Makes unilateral decisions
	Encourages open dialogue	Dominates conversations
	Shares leadership when appropriate	Ignores quieter or dissenting voices
RECOGNITION	Regularly celebrates wins and contributions	Only praises big outcomes
	Acknowledges effort, not just results	Ignores team accomplishments
	Personalizes recognition to the individual	Makes recognition transactional or inconsistent

ALIGNMENT

Value	Aligned Behavior	Misaligned Behavior
COURAGE	Addresses difficult issues directly	Avoids conflict
	Says what needs to be said with care and clarity	Sugarcoats feedback
	Makes tough decisions that align with values	Fails to speak up for what's right
GROWTH	Seeks feedback proactively	Avoids risk or change
	Embraces challenges and discomfort	Resists feedback
	Models continuous learning	Prioritizes ease or routine over progress
FAIRNESS	Applies standards and consequences consistently	Shows favoritism
	Examines and challenges personal bias	Uses inconsistent standards
	Ensures all voices are considered in decision-making	Makes decisions based on personal preference

Value	Aligned Behavior	Misaligned Behavior
RESPECT	Listens without interrupting or dismissing	Interrupts or talks over others
RESPECT	Treats all team members with dignity, regardless of role	Uses sarcasm or dismissive tones
RESPECT	Demonstrates appreciation for diverse perspectives	Plays down input from "lower-level" employees
ADAPTABILITY	Adjusts plans when conditions change	Rigidly sticks to plans, even when they're no longer working
ADAPTABILITY	Stays calm in uncertainty	Panics or resists when change happens
ADAPTABILITY	Is open to new ideas or better ways of doing things	Shuts down suggestions or innovation
SERVICE	Looks for ways to support and empower others	Focuses on personal gain or image
SERVICE	Makes decisions that benefit the team or organization, not just self	Neglects to invest time in team development
SERVICE	Puts team needs ahead of ego	Prioritizes visibility over meaningful contribution

ALIGNMENT

REFLECTION QUESTIONS

Looking at the values in the table, which ones do you consider important to your leadership?

_____

_____

_____

Which of those values do you *think* you consistently live out through your behavior (your actual values)?

_____

_____

_____

Which ones feel more aspirational—values you believe in or want to be known for but don't consistently act on yet?

_____

_____

_____

What would it look like to close the gap between those two?

_____

_____

_____

Actions: How Can You Practice What You Preach?

While defining values is easy in theory, the real test comes in practice, especially under pressure. When everything's going well, it's not hard to lead in alignment with what we say matters. When my team is thriving, fully trained, engaged, and delivering great results, it's easy to say I value learning and development. Of course I do! But leadership isn't lived in ideal conditions. It's lived in calendars, conversations, and especially in the moments when we're tired, overwhelmed, or frustrated.

So what happens when my team isn't meeting expectations right away? Do I still value growth, or do I default to control and urgency? That's where the gap shows up between the values I claim and the values I actually lead from.

Let's make this practical. If you say you value collaboration, what does that actually look like? How would someone on your team know? As leaders, we need to define our values not just in aspirational or abstract terms but in actions.

Instead of saying, "I value collaboration," show that you value collaboration through your behavior so that you can say you value it with a straight face. That might sound like:

- "I seek input from my team before making major decisions."

- "I encourage open discussion, even when opinions differ from mine."
- "I acknowledge and act on feedback rather than dismissing it."

When our values don't translate into clear, observable behaviors, they remain aspirational rather than lived. Understanding your motivations and values is a critical first step. But the real challenge lies in bringing our motivations and values to life through consistent, aligned action.

As you've likely learned the hard way, as I have many a time, we don't get credit for our intentions in most cases. We get credit for our impact. We don't just get to declare what we value or what motivates us. We have to prove it through our behavior. When our values, motivations, and actions are in harmony, we build credibility, trust, and consistency. But when there's a disconnect, our teams notice. Over time, our contradictions erode trust, and our words lose their weight. And when that happens, our team members are texting each other during team meetings about how clueless we are about ourselves. And we definitely don't want that.

Exercises to Bring Your Values and Motivations into Alignment

Most leaders don't wake up in the morning planning to act out of alignment with their values. But the pace of leadership, the pressure to perform, and the pull of old habits make misalignment the easier path. We don't drift into congruence. We choose it. These simple but intentional practices will help you slow down, reflect, and recalibrate. Don't get overwhelmed, and don't try to do all of these at the same time. Pick one to start, and watch what happens.

- ☐ **The Values Audit:** Over the next week, keep a leadership journal. Each day, reflect on your key leadership interactions and decisions. Ask yourself: Did my actions align with my core values? If not, why? What would I do differently next time?

- ☐ **Behavior Mapping:** Choose one of your stated leadership values (e.g., transparency, recognition, accountability). List two to three specific behaviors that should reflect that value. Then, track whether those behaviors show up consistently in your leadership. If they don't, brainstorm small changes to integrate them into your leadership approach.

- ☐ **The "Motivation in Action" Reflection:** Think about a recent leadership decision you made. What was the driving motivation behind it? (E.g., did you take control because it felt safer? Did you defer to others because you wanted to be liked?) Ask yourself: Does this motivation align with the leader I want to be? Then, identify one small adjustment that would bring your motivation and values into better alignment next time.

- ☐ **The Leadership Lens Exercise:** Imagine a trusted colleague or mentor is evaluating your leadership from the outside. What would they say about how well your actions align with your values and motivations? Would they see consistency between what you say you care about and how you show up every day?

- ☐ **The Leadership Legacy Letter:** Write a letter to yourself from five years in the future. Describe the kind of leader you became, the values you lived out, and the impact you had on your team. What needs to change today to align your leadership with that vision?

On a personal note, it's hard for me to know that I won't

get to sit down one-on-one with you to unpack your insights. If you're so inclined, shoot me an email at leanne@leannelagasse.com and let me know what you're learning about yourself, whether through one of these exercises or those to come in the rest of the book. I would love to hear how you're learning and growing.

Carrying on now.

Bringing your motivations, values, and actions into harmony is about awareness and intentionality, not perfection. The best leaders don't always get it right but consistently reflect, adjust, and grow through the challenges. The more congruently you lead, the more trust you'll build with your team and the more fulfilled you'll feel in your leadership role.

The real test of leadership congruence is how we apply that awareness in our daily interactions, especially when facing challenges, pressure, or competing priorities.

My coaching client, Josiah, who incorrectly assumed he was a collaborative leader, turned his situation around big-time once he learned there was a big gap between how he thought he was showing up and how his team members actually experienced him. After sharing the 360-review feedback with his team, he committed to examining his leadership behaviors and rhythms to identify areas for more collaborative communication and decision-making. He incorporated techniques like "brainwriting" in team meetings, where all team members write their ideas and opinions before discussion and deliberation begin. He created more upward communication channels for team members to share their perspectives. He made sure to add more context to his decision-making communication.

As a result, his team members pointed out the "collaborative team environment" in his next 360 review. He was pumped, and so was I. He had put in the work to close the gap and become a more congruent leader. The transformation didn't happen overnight, but it happened because he was willing to examine the gap and take action.

You can do that too.

Bringing It Home

Aligning our motivations, values, and actions is a daily practice and takes awareness, honesty, and a willingness to make adjustments when we drift. In congruent leadership, we notice when something feels off, reflect on what matters most, and choose to realign with purpose.

When we lead in a way that reflects what we truly care about, we build deeper trust with our teams. We create consistency, credibility, and clarity in our leadership. That kind of alignment strengthens both our impact and our connection to the people we lead.

So far, we've focused on what drives us and what we stand for. In the next chapter, we'll explore what we naturally do well. Pillar Three invites us to take inventory of our unique strengths and understand how they influence the way we lead. Because when we understand and invest in our talents, we can lead with greater clarity, confidence, and intention.

Let's turn the page and explore what happens when we lead from our strengths.

ALIGNMENT

REFLECTION QUESTIONS

To assess whether you're leading in alignment with your values and motivations, ask yourself:

Where do my daily actions reinforce my stated values? Can I point to specific behaviors that consistently demonstrate what I say I believe?

_____

_____

_____

Where do I feel tension or frustration in my leadership? Does it stem from acting in ways that conflict with my deeper values or motivations?

_____

_____

_____

When do I feel most engaged and energized as a leader? What patterns emerge in those moments that align with my core motivations?

_____

_____

_____

What feedback have I received that suggests I'm not living out my values? Are there areas where my team experiences me differently than I see myself?

_____

_____

_____

Am I making leadership decisions based on external pressures, expectations, or fears rather than my true motivations and values? If so, what needs to change?

_____

_____

_____

ALIGNMENT

MOTIVATIONS:
Why am I leading? What's driving me?

_____

_____

_____

VALUES:
What do I stand for?

_____

_____

_____

ACTIONS:
How am I actually showing up?

_____

_____

_____

This simple reflection is one I revisit regularly. Grab a sticky note, journal page, or whiteboard and ask yourself: *Why am I leading? What do I stand for? How am I showing up?*

PILLAR THREE

STRENGTHS

CHAPTER 5

Leverage Your Talents and Strengths

Key Question: *What would change in your leadership if you fully embraced and leveraged your natural talents and strengths?*

OUR BEST POTENTIAL FOR leadership excellence lies in our areas of natural talent and strength. This is, in fact, another hill I will die on. That conviction isn't *just* based on research or my coaching and training experience—it's also deeply personal to me. Discovering my own strengths and choosing to double down on them changed the trajectory of my career and my confidence. It helped me stop trying to lead like someone else and start showing up with more clarity, authenticity, and purpose. It gave me permission to lead like *me*.

That's what I want for you too, because it's a transformational shift that I've seen happen over and over again in the lives of the leaders I work with. When you stop trying to contort yourself into someone else's mold, whether it's a former boss, a charismatic peer, or some mythical version of "what a leader should be," you free up your energy to lead from a place of clarity and grounded confidence. You begin to notice the specific ways your strengths already influence your leadership, and you gain language to build on them intentionally.

If values alignment is the compass that keeps you on course, your talents and strengths are the vehicle that gets you where you need to go. They shape how you make decisions, approach challenges, and interact with others. They determine the hills you will die on too.

This is the essence of Pillar Three: Leverage Your Talents and Strengths, which is all about learning to use what comes most naturally to you as an advantage, rather than trying to lead like someone else. The most effective leaders use their strengths with precision. They understand where they bring the most value, how to communicate their strengths to others, and how to continuously refine them.

This chapter will help you take a clear-eyed look at your strengths and explore how to fully leverage them in your leadership. Whether you are someone who instinctively rallies a team around a vision, sees patterns and solutions others miss, or finds ways to optimize and refine processes, your leadership success will be defined by maximizing what you already do best.

Don't Try to Be Everything: Your Talents and Strengths Are Key to Your Leadership Success

Most of us have been conditioned to believe that becoming a great leader means becoming more *well-rounded*. The idea seems logical at first. If we could just smooth out our rough edges and get better at the things we're naturally bad at, we'd be unstoppable.

We'll say, "If only I were a more strategic leader," or "I wish I had as much charisma as so-and-so." Because of this thinking, many leadership development efforts focus on shoring up weaknesses. Performance reviews zero in on gaps and areas for improvement. Development plans revolve around "fixing" deficiencies. Even well-meaning managers often spend more time coaching people on what they lack rather than amplifying what they already do best.

Now, that all sounds great in theory, but consider the following:

- When was the last time you saw someone chronically disorganized become a master of structure and precision?

- When was the last time you saw someone who finds data mind-numbing suddenly transform into an analytical wizard, effortlessly spotting patterns in complex reports?

What about *your* weaknesses? Have you tried to shore them up for years, maybe your entire life? Maybe you've grown a bit here or there but, if you're like most people, you haven't experienced a colossal transformation yet.

Don't get me wrong. I believe in growth and working through our challenges. Of course, we can strengthen our weaker areas, at least to some extent. But the best leaders don't achieve success by trying to be *everything*. They succeed by leaning hard into what they already do well and by recognizing their natural talents and turning them into refined, powerful strengths.

The Case for Strengths-Based Leadership

At its core, *strengths-based leadership* is the intentional practice of identifying, developing, and deploying your most natural talents in ways that drive personal effectiveness and team success. Rather than focusing primarily on fixing weaknesses, it prioritizes building on what already works. As Gallup research consistently shows, leaders who focus on their strengths are more engaged, productive, and likely to retain team members compared to those who don't.[28] In fact, when individuals use their strengths daily, they're six times more likely to be engaged at work.

I'm going to keep going, for good measure, and because this is such great news for the discouraged leader. Research also shows that when leaders play to their strengths, they experience greater confidence, resilience, and motivation, and report a higher quality of life.

This is great news for our team members too, because teams led by strengths-focused leaders report higher productivity, stronger trust, and a more collaborative culture. Sounds like a no brainer, yes? Yet, too many leaders overlook this truth, convinced they need to "round themselves out" before they can lead effectively. But the reality is, leadership success isn't about becoming balanced—it's about becoming potent.

Consider Jordan, a leader known for her ability to think big, rally a team around a vision, and drive innovation. However, after her last 360 review, she noticed feedback about her lack of attention to detail and inconsistent follow-through on administrative tasks.

Determined to become more well-rounded, Jordan threw herself into fixing these "weaknesses." She signed up for productivity courses, bought a few organization and time management books, and tried to pull herself up by her bootstraps and implement what she learned. The result? She was exhausted, frustrated, and no more effective than before. Her team noticed she seemed distracted and less energized. The innovative spark that used to light up the team's brainstorming meetings? Dimming fast.

The problem was that she was pouring her energy into areas that would never be her zone of genius. Instead of delegating or partnering with someone strong in execution, she was trying to become someone she wasn't. In the process, she was underusing the very strengths that had made her successful in the first place. That's the trap many leaders fall into: overcorrecting for our gaps instead of doubling down on our gifts. Imagine if instead of spending the bulk of your energy compensating for what you lack, you focused on refining what already sets you apart.

It bears repeating. As leaders, we don't need to be *everything*. We can't be everything and, actually, we will wear ourselves out quickly if we try.

And yet, despite all the research and real-life examples, I still hear this all the time: "But if we only focus on strengths, aren't we just ignoring our weaknesses?" Or "Isn't this just sugar-coating the hard stuff?" Honestly, those assumptions drive me a little bit bonkers, not because people are asking in bad faith, but because strengths-based leadership isn't about pretending our weaknesses don't exist or adopting a toxic positivity mindset.

Emphasizing strengths doesn't mean we turn a blind eye to our areas of vulnerability. Instead, it means we approach leadership with a realistic and strategic mindset, acknowledging that while weaknesses are part of the equation, they should not be the primary focus of our growth. A strengths-based approach helps leaders work within their natural capabilities while also developing strategies to manage or mitigate their weaker areas. This isn't about avoiding growth. It's about focusing energy where it yields the highest return while ensuring that weaknesses don't derail leadership effectiveness.

REFLECTION QUESTIONS

When have you felt pressured to "fix" a weakness rather than focus on a strength? How did that impact your energy, confidence, or effectiveness?

_____

_____

_____

Think about a time when you tried to lead in a way that didn't feel natural to you. What was the outcome? How did it feel compared to when you leaned into your strengths?

_____

_____

_____

Turn Up the Volume on What Works

If you've ever felt stuck trying to be a kind of leader you're not, welcome to the club. Here's the good news: Your natural strengths already hold the key to meaningful progress. Earlier in this book, we discussed the concept of locus of control—whether you see yourself as having control over your circumstances (*internal locus of control*) or believe external forces dictate your outcomes (*external locus of control*). Strengths-based leadership begins with ownership and is grounded in the belief that it's our responsibility to develop and apply our talents. That's why this approach is so closely tied to an internal locus of control. Leaders who thrive choose to use their strengths intentionally. They take initiative, direct their energy with purpose, and actively shape the kind of leader they're becoming. When we fully own our strengths, name them, trust them, and put them to work, we start to see real transformation in our leadership.

What Happens When You Own Your Strengths?

When leaders take full ownership of their strengths, a few key things happen:

1. They develop their strengths with intention. They don't assume that because something comes naturally, they have nothing left to learn. They refine their talents, practice them, and push themselves to grow.

2. They apply their strengths strategically. They look for opportunities to direct their strengths toward their biggest leadership challenges.

3. They create greater impact. When strengths are used with intentionality, they lead to tangible results. Leaders who fully own their strengths make better decisions, lead more effectively, and inspire trust in those around them.

What would shift if you stopped trying to lead like

someone else and started turning up the volume on what already makes you powerful? If you're ready to turn up that volume, the first step is getting clear on what you're actually working with—your most natural talents and how they show up in your leadership.

Identifying Your Talents and Strengths

Helping people discover their talents and strengths is one of the most energizing activities in my life. Uncovering uniqueness in others has always come naturally to me. Discovering what makes someone thrive and flourish fills my cup.

And I've always been this way. Remember my nickname? *The Nose.*

I bring it up again to share another truth about talent:

There's a difference between *having* talent and *using* it well. The Gallup Organization defines talent as "naturally recurring patterns of thought, feeling, or behavior, that can be productively applied."[29] The key words here? *Can be.* Talents don't automatically become strengths. We've all known someone with natural talent, whether in leadership, communication, problem-solving, or creativity, who never quite manages to turn that talent into something meaningful. Maybe they rely on it too casually, assuming it will always be there when needed. Maybe they fail to develop it, leaving it as raw potential rather than a refined ability. Maybe they even misuse it, applying it in ways that don't serve them or their team well.

A *strength* results from intentionally developed talent that is directed toward productive outcomes. Strengths don't emerge overnight but are built through repeated use, refinement, and growth and enable us to consistently create value, drive results, and positively impact the people around us.

Just because we have a talent doesn't mean we're using

it effectively. And just because something comes naturally doesn't mean it's being applied in a way that serves others, our mission, or our leadership goals. A natural ability can be useful without being fully developed. You may be naturally persuasive, but without learning when and how to apply that persuasion, it can feel like pressure instead of influence. You might be wired to think strategically, but your ideas won't drive results if you don't pair that with action. A true strength is not just something you're good at. It's something you've honed to deliver consistent, positive outcomes.

My son, Eli, who gave me permission to share this story, was born competitive. From the moment he discovered he could compare his progress to the progress of others, he has gained energy from playing the game and trying to win. My husband and I figured out early in his toddler years that we could motivate him to do most things if we turned it into a race or a win-lose scenario. That's his talent at work—a natural pattern of thinking that drives him to compete and compare.

But you might anticipate where I'm headed next. While Eli's natural patterns of thinking, feeling, and behaving lent themselves to a love of competition, he wasn't born with the ability to leverage it as a strength. For example, when we tried to play board games as a family when he was younger, all was well when he was winning. But if he started to lose, one of two things usually happened: (1) He would quit before the game was over, or (2) He would become emotionally dysregulated and lose his temper. Did he occasionally turn over the board game in anger? Did his temper sometimes impact the rest of us and our level of enjoyment? Yes, yes, it did. While his natural talent was at work, he was not yet using that talent well.

Over time, Eli has invested in that raw talent and uses it much more productively now, most times in service to a big goal, mission, and his teammates. He's gotten the reps in over the years, both in winning and losing, to learn how to better apply the talent to the outcomes he's after. Eli's story reminds us that when we work to refine our natural talents, they can become powerful tools. Today, he's more aware of this pattern of thinking. He reflects on how he's using it regularly. That didn't happen overnight, and yes, he sometimes still struggles with it today.

It's ironic though, isn't it? The strengths that come most naturally to us are often the ones we fail to recognize or value. Because they feel effortless, we assume they're nothing special. Meanwhile, we look at other people or leaders, admiring their ability to think on their feet, build instant rapport, or make sense of complexity, and we wish we had *their* superpowers.

In workshops, I often ask a simple question: Who here can usually figure out the plot of a movie way before everyone else? Without fail, a handful of people smirk, raise their hands, and shrug like it's no big deal. They'll say, "Well, yeah, but it's always *sooo* obvious. I mean, I can't not see it."

But that's where I stop them to point out, often self-deprecatingly, "Well, it's that obvious to *you*, while people like *me* are always surprised at the end of the movie."

The people who can spot the twists early assume that everyone else can too. They don't realize that for most people, those same plot points remain a mystery until the final reveal. What feels effortless to them isn't effortless for everyone. It's a natural ability, something wired into the way they process patterns, anticipate outcomes, or read between the lines.

We all do this with our own strengths. When something comes naturally to us, we assume that ability must be easy for everyone. We downplay it, dismiss it, or even feel it doesn't "count" as a real skill because it doesn't feel hard. But that's the mistake. Just because something is easy for *you* doesn't mean it's easy for *everyone*. What comes naturally to you is unique.

And yet, instead of embracing that, we compare. And because I believe that a drive for competition and comparison can be used as a leadership strength, I want to make an important distinction here. It's one thing to compare for the sake of excellence, but it's another to compare because you wish you were someone else. A leader who is deeply intuitive about people might wish they were more data-driven and analytical. A leader who can naturally distill complex ideas into clear, persuasive messages might envy those who thrive in ambiguity and rapid problem-solving. A leader who builds deep trust through one-on-one connections might feel like they're "not dynamic enough" compared to someone with a big, charismatic stage presence.

Comparison keeps us stuck. It makes us think that our natural way of leading isn't enough. But the best leaders don't waste energy trying to be someone they're not. They learn to fully embrace the way they lead best. The challenge isn't about whether or not you have talents and strengths but whether you'll own the ones you do have. Because the truth is, someone else looks at you, wishing they have what you so easily overlook.

REFLECTION QUESTION

What comes so naturally to you that you barely notice it, but others frequently point it out or ask for your help with it?

_____

_____

_____

If you're not quite sure, you're not alone. In the next section, we'll look at a few practical ways to uncover those hidden strengths and bring them into the light.

Indicators of Your Most Natural Talents

Here are a few key ways to recognize your talents and strengths in action:

- **When do you feel most energized, productive, and effective?** Strengths typically energize us. Think about the moments in your work where you feel fully engaged, when time flies by, when you leave a meeting feeling more energized than when you walked in, or when you're in a flow state. Those moments often point to strengths at work.

- **What do others naturally rely on you for?** Pay attention to what people consistently ask for your help with. Are you the person others turn to when they need someone to make sense of a complex situation? Are you the person people seek out when they need a calm, measured perspective in a high-stakes conversation? These patterns can reveal where you naturally bring value.

- **What's something you can't help but do, even when you're not trying?** Some strengths show up whether we intend them to or not. Maybe you can't walk into a room without instinctively noticing group dynamics and tensions. Maybe you naturally break big-picture ideas into structured plans without thinking about it. Maybe you can't *not* connect the dots between seemingly unrelated pieces of information. These tendencies are often clues to deep-rooted strengths that, when developed, can become powerful leadership tools.

Identifying your strengths helps you recognize what is already there and learn how to refine and aim it effectively.

REFLECTION QUESTIONS

What are a few moments when you felt completely in your element as a leader?

_____

_____

_____

Think about the last time you finished a task or conversation and felt more energized than when you started. What were you doing? What does that say about what lights you up?

_____

_____

_____

A Guide to Leadership Strengths

If you're like me, you love a good list, especially one that helps put language to what you've always sensed about yourself. Before we dive into this next part, let's get our minds right again. We're not meant to have all these strengths. My hope is that as you scan the list on the following pages, you'll spot a few that feel like home. A few that make you think, *Oh, that's me. I just didn't have the words for it until now.*

Thinking and Problem-Solving Strengths

These strengths impact how you process information, make decisions, and approach complex challenges.

THINKING AND PROBLEM-SOLVING STRENGTHS	
Pattern Recognition	Quickly identifying trends, connections, and insights that others miss.
Creative Problem-Solving	Seeing unconventional solutions and generating innovative approaches.
Logical Structuring	Breaking down complex issues into clear, actionable steps.
Big-Picture Thinking	Focusing on long-term vision and broad organizational impact.
Contextual Awareness	Understanding historical trends and past experiences to inform decisions.
Data-Driven Decision-Making	Relying on evidence, numbers, and analysis to make sound judgments.
Anticipatory Thinking	Predicting future obstacles and preparing for them proactively.
Simplification and Synthesis	Distilling complex information into simple, digestible insights.
Curiosity and Inquiry	Asking thoughtful questions to uncover deeper truths.
Systems Thinking	Seeing how different pieces fit together within a larger framework.

People and Relationship Strengths

These strengths impact how you connect, inspire, and influence those around you.

PEOPLE AND RELATIONSHIP STRENGTHS	
Connector	Building relationships and networks that create opportunities for collaboration.
Motivator	Energizing and inspiring people to take action toward a shared goal.
Empathetic Listener	Understanding others' emotions, perspectives, and unspoken concerns.
Talent Spotter	Recognizing potential in people and helping them develop.
Bridge Builder	Uniting people across different teams, perspectives, or backgrounds.
Trust Builder	Creating a culture of psychological safety and mutual respect.
Personalized Leadership	Adjusting your approach based on individuals' unique talents and needs.
Conflict Navigator	Managing disagreements with grace and turning them into opportunities for growth.
Emotional Agility	Responding appropriately to emotional cues in a dynamic environment.
Storytelling Influence	Using compelling narratives to create connection and drive action.

Execution and Productivity Strengths

These strengths drive momentum, efficiency, and results.

EXECUTION AND PRODUCTIVITY STRENGTHS	
Optimizer	Continuously improving systems, processes, and workflows for maximum impact.
Follow-Through	Ensuring commitments, projects, and goals are executed reliably.
High Standards	Pushing for excellence in quality, efficiency, or results.
Crisis Clarity	Remaining calm and making sound decisions under pressure.
Proactive Ownership	Anticipating needs and taking responsibility before being asked.
Time Maximization	Efficiently managing priorities and optimizing productivity.
Resilience and Endurance	Maintaining focus and energy through setbacks and challenges.
Operational Precision	Mastering details, logistics, and execution to ensure flawless delivery.
Adaptability	Adjusting quickly and effectively when plans, conditions, or expectations change.
Resourcefulness	Finding creative solutions even when time, money, or support is limited.

Communication and Influence Strengths

These strengths influence how you share ideas, shape perspectives, and mobilize others toward action.

COMMUNICATION AND INFLUENCE STRENGTHS	
Persuasive Storytelling	Framing messages in ways that emotionally resonate and inspire.
Clarity in Complexity	Making intricate ideas simple, understandable, and actionable.
Presence and Gravitas	Commanding attention, credibility, and respect in a room.
Adaptable Communication	Tailoring tone, style, and approach to different audiences.
Thought Leadership	Articulating unique insights that shape perspectives and drive change.
Collaboration Catalyst	Encouraging cross-functional teamwork and cooperative problem-solving.
Sensemaking	Helping others interpret ambiguous situations and find direction.
Diplomacy and Tact	Managing delicate situations with discretion, balance, and respect.
Constructive Challenger	Asking the right questions to push for better solutions and approaches.
Feedback Champion	Giving and receiving feedback in a way that fosters learning and growth.

Innovation and Future-Oriented Strengths

These strengths help leaders drive progress, anticipate opportunities, and push boundaries.

INNOVATION AND FUTURE-ORIENTED STRENGTHS	
Visionary Thinking	Seeing and shaping the future with clarity and confidence.
Risk Assessment	Balancing bold ideas with thoughtful evaluation of potential pitfalls.
Change Agility	Embracing transformation and helping others navigate it successfully.
Disruptive Thinking	Challenging the status quo and pushing for fresh approaches.
Opportunity Spotting	Recognizing untapped potential in ideas, markets, or talent.
Foresight and Trend Awareness	Anticipating shifts in the industry and positioning accordingly.
Idea Amplification	Taking rough concepts and refining them into something actionable.
Inventiveness	Designing new products, services, or strategies to drive differentiation.
Resilient Experimentation	Willing to test new approaches, learn from failure, and iterate.
Cross-Disciplinary Thinking	Drawing insights from multiple fields to innovate.

A Note on the Strength Tables: If you're looking for additional insights into your natural talents, a variety of well-researched assessments help individuals identify and maximize their strengths. Tools like Gallup's CliftonStrengths Assessment, the VIA Character Strengths Survey, and Hogan Assessments offer structured ways to explore patterns in your thinking, behavior, and leadership approach. While no assessment can fully define you, they can provide a helpful starting point for reflection and growth.

A Strengths-Based Mindset: Same Outcomes, Different Methods

If one of the goals of leadership is to influence, inspire, and drive results, there is no single way to get there. Strengths-based leadership allows you to approach challenges in a way that aligns with how *you* work best. To lead like *you*.

- A leader who thrives on deep, meaningful conversations might build team buy-in through one-on-one discussions, while a high-energy, fast-moving leader might inspire a room with a compelling vision and momentum.

- A highly detail-oriented leader might drive success through meticulous planning and flawless execution, while a big-picture thinker might succeed by rallying people around the broader vision and then delegating the details.

- A leader who is naturally structured and disciplined might create consistency through systems and processes. In contrast, a leader who thrives in adaptability might bring stability by helping others easily navigate change.

None of these approaches are better than the others. They are simply different paths to the same outcome. The key is recognizing what *your* natural path is and using it intentionally to lead effectively. One of the biggest benefits of a strengths-based mindset is clarity. When you know where you bring the most value, you stop wasting energy trying to be everything to everyone. Instead of feeling pressure to lead like someone else, you focus on maximizing the strengths that already exist within you. You find the intersection between what you do best and what your team or organization needs most, and that's where your greatest impact happens.

Leaders who embrace their strengths with confidence, and apply them with intentionality, feel more energized and engaged, and create better results, stronger teams, and more fulfilling careers. Strengths are something you *use*. And when you use them well, they become your greatest asset.

But here's where many leaders get stuck: We assume that the path to success should look the same for everyone. The truth is that what contributes to someone else's leadership success may or may not be the way for me too. In fact, what makes someone else successful might be a wildly unsuccessful method for me. We don't need to lead the same way to achieve success. We can get to the same outcomes using different methods.

Imagine two department heads, Alex and Jordan, who are both tasked with improving team performance. Alex is highly relational. He thrives on building trust, fostering collaboration, and motivating people through connection. Throughout his life, people have affirmed his relationship-building talents, and he has developed a reputation for his people intelligence.

Jordan, however, is highly analytical. She excels at data-driven decision-making, problem-solving, and optimizing systems for efficiency. For as long as she can remember, she was capable of logical reasoning and deducing the best path forward based on the available data.

Both Alex and Jordan need to achieve similar results. They will be held accountable for their efforts. Because both are rooted in a strengths-based approach, their methods will vary.

Alex hosts regular one-on-one check-ins to understand team members' challenges, provides personal encouragement, and creates a more engaging team culture. By focusing on morale and relationships, team productivity improves because employees feel valued and supported. They are bought in because they trust Alex's leadership.

Meanwhile, Jordan tackles the challenge by analyzing workflow bottlenecks, adjusting processes, and setting clear KPIs to measure success. By optimizing efficiency and eliminating unnecessary steps, team productivity improves because employees have better tools and clearer direction. But guess what? Jordan's team is also bought in because they trust her leadership.

Both leaders achieve the goal in a way that aligns with their natural strengths. Neither approach is "better," but each leader leverages what they do best to drive results. Knowing where you bring value means aligning your strengths with leadership opportunities that make the best use of them. It also means being aware of when you are operating outside your natural zone of excellence. When leaders try to contribute in ways that don't align with their strengths, they risk burnout, frustration, and missed opportunities to create real impact.

The key is to recognize the situations where your strengths are most useful and seek them out. Whether it's strategy, execution, people development, or innovation, your leadership effectiveness increases when you intentionally apply your strengths to the right challenges. Instead of spreading yourself thin across every demand, you can focus on the areas where you can make the biggest difference, areas where your leadership feels both natural and powerful.

REFLECTION QUESTION

What's one leadership result you're working toward right now, and what strength could you lean into to get there in your own way?

_____

_____

_____

Making Your Strengths Work for You

It was my first time presenting at a large HR conference. Although I had plenty of previous experience presenting—I was the public speaking director at a large university, for heaven's sake—I felt anxious about how this new audience would perceive me. I was delivering a presentation on employee onboarding, specifically how organizations can craft messages to boost engagement and retention.

When I arrived, I felt positive-ish about my talk. My slide deck was nearly done, and I decided to sit in on another session about onboarding, hoping to gauge the audience's reactions and get a feel for the speakers. But when I walked in, my heart sank. The room was packed, standing room only. Immediately, self-doubt kicked in: Why would anyone come to my session tomorrow if they were clearly so excited about this one?

The presenter was polished, experienced, and confident. She'd appeared on the *Today Show*, authored several books, and worked with high-profile clients. As she spoke, sharing many of the same research points I'd planned to cover, I shrank in my chair. For forty-five minutes, my anxiety grew. I became convinced that compared to her, I had nothing meaningful to offer. I left the session feeling sorry for myself, certain my relative inexperience as a consultant would prevent the audience from taking me seriously. The imposter syndrome was strong. I was sure everyone would see right through me.

Back in my hotel room, my first instinct (right or wrong) was to completely rewrite my presentation. Initially, the only thought in my mind was: *I have to come up with something better than hers.* But as I stared at my slide deck, I felt stuck and overwhelmed. How could I possibly measure up?

Then, suddenly, like a ton of obvious bricks, I had a thought. Instead of focusing on what this presenter had done so well, I asked myself a different question: *What are the specific things I do very well? What unique skills do I bring as a speaker? How can I differentiate my session from hers so that attendees get great value?*

The answer was immediate: I'm a *teacher*. I have a unique ability to facilitate meaningful learning and dynamic discussions. I excel at engaging people in conversations and crafting thoughtful questions. My natural strength is creating a vibrant, interactive classroom environment.

So, that's what I did. I completely reworked my session, shaping it into a facilitated classroom-style experience. I built in discussion questions, allowed space for participants to share their ideas and challenges, and still included all the important research and actionable strategies from my original slides.

The result? Based on my session evaluations, attendees

loved it. My session was rated as one of the top three at the entire conference. I share this to illustrate a powerful truth: Had I stuck with my original plan—trying to mimic someone else's style—I never would have achieved that outcome. My success came from leaning into what made me uniquely valuable.

Yes, I recognize the irony. I've built my career around strengths-based development and leadership. However, at that moment, I struggled to see clearly. This is why carving out intentional time for reflection and mindfulness matters. A strengths-based mindset is about believing that our best path to success comes from amplifying the strengths we already have.

How Do We Develop Our Talents into Leadership Strengths?

Turning talent into leadership strengths takes deliberate use, real-world testing, and the humility to keep growing. Here are some practical things you can do:

Intentionally Flex Your Talent Muscles

A leader with a natural ability to build rapport might find connecting with people in casual conversations easy to do, but that doesn't mean they have fully developed the ability to inspire trust, navigate difficult relationships, or foster deep engagement within a team. Along those same lines, someone with an intuitive ability to see patterns in data may struggle to communicate those insights in a way that drives action. Talent alone isn't enough—it must be shaped, tested, and refined in real-world leadership situations.

One of the most effective ways to develop a strength is through intentional practice. Leaders grow by actively using their strengths in different contexts similar to how an athlete refines their technique through repetition and adjustment. A leader with a gift for resourcefulness might challenge themselves to streamline a struggling process or optimize team workflows. A naturally strategic thinker might practice articulating their vision in a way that helps others buy in and execute the plan.

To continue developing, look for opportunities to apply your strengths deliberately, especially in situations that push you outside your comfort zone. Strengths grow through real application and not passive awareness. I often tell my coaching clients to say yes to more opportunities that align with their talents, even if those opportunities feel challenging, because the stretching in those areas will have a compounding effect due to their already existing talent in that area.

Pair Talents with Skill Development

Even the most natural talents need backup. I've coached leaders who could spot the big picture from a mile away but got tripped up trying to translate their vision into next steps. And that's okay. This doesn't mean your strength isn't valid, but it may need a little support to do its best work. Think of it this way: Your strengths are the stars of the show, but sometimes they need a strong supporting cast. Someone who is exceptional at personal relationships, for instance, might amplify that strength by learning techniques in influence, conflict resolution, or negotiation—skills that help their relational intelligence land with even greater impact.

That's why it's so important to recognize where your strengths shine on their own, and where they might benefit from a few well-placed sidekicks. Strengths don't exist in isolation. They are most powerful when combined with other competencies that enhance their impact. A leader who excels in problem-solving but lacks storytelling skills may struggle to gain buy-in for their ideas. A leader who thrives on precision and order may need to cultivate adaptability to navigate unpredictable challenges. The most effective leaders recognize that their strengths are not fixed; they can be expanded, refined, and made even more impactful by acquiring complementary skills.

Refine Your Strengths Through Feedback

Raw talent can be powerful, but without feedback and intentional refinement, it can lead to blind spots or unintended consequences. (We'll dig into this more in the next chapter, by the way.) One of the biggest mistakes leaders make is assuming that because something comes naturally to them, they're already using it well. Leaders who are highly results-oriented may overlook the emotional needs of their team. Those with a natural gift for big-picture thinking may dismiss practical details too quickly. The key to maximizing strengths is to understand when they are helping and when they need adjustment.

Feedback is one of the most valuable tools for this refinement and helps leaders see how their strengths land with others, where they are driving positive impact, and where they may need to be adapted. A leader who sees themselves as highly decisive might realize that their quick decision-making is unintentionally shutting down team discussions. Another leader who prides themselves on being highly organized may find that their structured approach feels rigid to those who need more flexibility.

The best leaders stay curious about their impact, remain open to feedback, and fine-tune their approach. They learn when to dial a strength up, when to pull it back, and how to aim it with greater precision.

Developing talents into strengths is an ongoing practice.

The more intentionally we hone our abilities, the more consistently we'll achieve the outcomes we're working toward. As we gather feedback and stay engaged with how others experience our leadership, we sharpen the edges of our natural abilities.

Aim Your Strengths at the Leadership Outcomes You Need

While your strengths are powerful tools, their impact depends on how intentionally you use them. A hammer is excellent for driving nails but ineffective for cutting wood. Similarly, your strengths won't automatically lead to success unless you consciously direct them toward the outcomes you need.

Many leaders assume that simply knowing their strengths is enough. But awareness alone won't create results. What matters is how you *apply* your strengths to real challenges and opportunities. Strengths must be aimed at making a meaningful impact.

For example, a leader with strong strategic thinking skills might naturally see patterns and anticipate challenges. However, if they don't intentionally use this ability to help their team plan ahead, their ability remains untapped potential. A leader with strong people skills might excel at creating trust and connection, but if they don't actively use that to align their team around shared goals, it's just an innate talent, and not a strength in action.

Effective leaders continuously ask themselves:

- How can I leverage my strengths to solve this problem?

- What adjustments do I need to make to ensure my strengths serve my team?

- Am I overusing or misapplying my strengths in a way that creates blind spots?

- Am I using this strength in a way that creates impact?
- Am I adapting my strengths to the needs of my team?

A talent by itself is merely potential. Leaders who actively direct their talents toward key outcomes, whether for efficiency, vision, or individualized leadership, turn them into a force multiplier for their team's success.

Start by asking yourself, "What is the outcome I need?" Then, you can discern the best ways to aim your talents and strengths at those outcomes.

When it comes to leadership outcomes like building trust, communicating care, solving problems, getting buy-in, or navigating change, there's no one "right way." Your unique strengths give you your own distinct path to success. For example, if your strength is relationship-building, you might get buy-in through personal conversations that emphasize mutual understanding. If you're analytical, you might lean into data or clear logic to demonstrate why an idea makes sense. Maybe you're naturally strategic and prefer to paint a vivid vision of the future to inspire others toward change. Or perhaps your talent for structure and execution helps you communicate care by reliably delivering on your commitments.

The point is your strengths aren't just "nice-to-haves." They are tools that can be strategically aimed at any leadership challenge. Your way of getting there won't look exactly like someone else's, and that's precisely why strengths-based leadership works.

Speak It So They Can See It: Owning and Articulating Your Strengths

Leaders frequently assume that their strengths are self-evident to others and that people will naturally notice their contributions and understand how they think and operate. But when you don't articulate your strengths, people fill in the blanks, and their assumptions might miss the mark and be inaccurate or unfavorable. The most effective leaders intentionally communicate their strengths, building credibility and trust in the process.

That being said, one of the biggest challenges in talking about strengths is striking the right balance between confidence and humility. Leaders who downplay their strengths risk being overlooked or underestimated, while those who overplay them can come across as prideful, egotistical, or self-serving. The key is to frame your strengths to highlight both your value and your commitment to the team's success.

Communicating strengths effectively means contextualizing them, clarifying why they matter and how they contribute to shared goals. Here are a few ways to communicate your strengths with both clarity and credibility:

- Share your specific contributions. Instead of vague statements like, "I'm good at building relationships," be specific: "One of the ways I add value is by fostering strong connections across departments, which has helped break down silos and improve collaboration between teams."

- When working with others, make your strengths explicit to foster better dynamics. If you thrive on structure and process, let your team know. You might say: "I tend to think in terms of systems and efficiency, so if we ever need help organizing a plan, I'd love to contribute."

- Help your team understand your working style and how you operate best. If you lead with a visionary mindset, you might say: "I naturally think a few steps ahead and love exploring new possibilities. If I ever seem to be pushing into the future too fast, let me know. I want to ensure I'm staying connected to what's most pressing now."

When we communicate openly and vulnerably about our talents and strengths as leaders, we create an environment of trust and authenticity. Sharing what comes most naturally to us helps our teams better understand our decisions and intentions while signaling to others that we possess genuine self-awareness. As a bonus, when we share openly about our strengths, we model congruence and encourage the same transparency and openness within our teams.

REFLECTION QUESTIONS

Do the people around you fully understand what you do best? How often do you communicate your strengths in a way that helps others see your value?

_____

_____

_____

Have you ever experienced a situation where your strengths were misunderstood? How could you communicate them more clearly to build trust and alignment?

_____

_____

_____

How might you invite your team to share their own strengths more openly, and what would that make possible in your collaboration?

_____

_____

_____

Strengths in Action

For years, Lisa believed that to be an effective leader, she had to become more like her peers. She admired her colleagues who were quick on their feet in brainstorming meetings, able to process new ideas rapidly, and contribute sharp insights in the moment. Lisa, on the other hand, needed time to process, reflect, and craft well-thought-out responses. She often left meetings frustrated, feeling like she wasn't adding value because she wasn't as fast as the others.

So, she tried to change. She forced herself to jump into conversations before she was ready, but her points often felt disjointed or half-formed. The more she pushed herself to mimic others' styles, the more disconnected she felt from her own strengths—and the less confidence she had in her leadership.

Everything shifted when Lisa started leaning into her actual strengths. She realized that her ability to think deeply, synthesize information, and provide well-reasoned insights was an asset—not a weakness. Instead of trying to force herself to speak up only to match her peers' speed, she started positioning herself as the leader who brought clarity and structure after the initial flood of ideas. She became the person who followed up with well-organized thoughts, synthesized conversations into actionable insights, and provided strategic direction when others were caught in reactive thinking.

The result? Her confidence soared, and her team started relying on her unique way of leading. Lisa stopped seeing her natural tendencies as limitations and started owning them as the powerful assets they were.

Strengths Are Our Greatest Asset—But They're Not the Whole Story

Lisa's transformation is a powerful example of leadership congruence. She stopped trying to lead like someone else and took ownership of her leadership by recognizing and refining what she did best. That's the heart of Pillar Three: Your strengths are powerful tools you can aim with purpose. When you use them intentionally, they become one of your greatest assets. When our actions reflect our inner wiring, our leadership resonates more deeply. The heart of strengths-based, congruent leadership is showing up in a way that's both true to ourselves and effective for others.

But what about the areas where we struggle? What do we do with the things that don't come naturally? In the next chapter, we'll explore Pillar Four and unpack what to do with our talent gaps, blind spots, and weaknesses to ensure they don't hold us back from leading with clarity, courage, and effectiveness.

PILLAR FOUR
LIMITATIONS

CHAPTER 6

Manage Your Talent Gaps, Weaknesses, and Blind Spots

Key Question: *How can you become a more trustworthy leader by managing what you lack, overuse, or can't always see?*

HERE'S AN UNCOMFORTABLE TRUTH about leadership: No matter how self-aware, well-intentioned, values-aligned, or strengths-focused we are, we will likely still wound our people occasionally. We'll miss details and dynamics. We'll lead from insecurity. We'll cause confusion, frustration, or disappointment without even realizing it. That's what makes leadership such a weighty responsibility we shouldn't take lightly or for granted.

This stage in the process is the beginning of a new kind of authentic leadership and focuses on owning the truth about what doesn't come as naturally. This pillar works in tandem with Pillar Three. Where Pillar Three invites us to name and leverage our strengths, Pillar Four calls us to manage what our strengths can't do and to lead wisely through the gaps they leave behind. Together, they build the clarity and self-awareness that congruent leadership requires.

Our talent gaps, weaknesses, and blind spots aren't necessarily leadership failures. They're often where our most meaningful growth opportunity lives. They're where trust is tested and earned. They're the places our strengths will either serve or sabotage us, depending on how willing we are to look in the mirror.

In the pages ahead, we'll explore how to identify and manage those gaps and make peace with the truth that being human is perhaps the most challenging part of leadership. This chapter is not about self-criticism or shame. It's about self-responsibility. It's the turn in your leadership where you move from celebrating what you do well to taking responsibility for what you don't, without letting it diminish your sense of worth or capability.

This chapter also isn't about "fixing our flaws." It's about becoming leaders who refuse to hide from them. Leaders who meet limitations with curiosity, not shame. Who take responsibility not just for what we intend to do but for the actual outcomes we get when we lead others. It's about holding both truths at once. Strength with humility. Confidence with curiosity. Ownership with openness.

That is the heart of Pillar Four: Manage Your Talent Gaps, Weaknesses, and Blind Spots. Because when you know what to do with your weaknesses, they stop being major liabilities. And when you learn to aim your strengths at your gaps, you become the kind of leader people trust.

Confronting Your Limits Through a Strengths-Based Lens

A strength that's not grounded in self-awareness can quietly sabotage the very outcomes you're trying to create. Imagine the leader who prides themselves on clarity, who might unintentionally shut down creativity and innovation. Or the leader who thrives on connection being so busy trying to keep the peace that they avoid hard conversations until trust erodes. Left unchecked, strengths don't just become neutral; they can become liabilities.

There's a reason many leaders resist this kind of self-examination; it's hard! It's painful to admit that your best qualities might also be hurting someone. But doing this work isn't a sign of weakness. It's the emotional labor of leadership, and the leaders who do it earn the trust of others.

Making Peace with What You're Not

We've already discussed the myth of the "well-rounded leader." This idea has heaped shame and guilt on many an outstanding leader. Contrary to the messages we often send ourselves, we don't need to be the most visionary *and* the most detail-oriented leader. We don't need to be the calmest presence in a crisis *and* the most high-energy motivator. We don't need to hold every strength in the book to be an extraordinary leader.

But it must be said: Making peace with our limitations doesn't mean we stop growing. It means we stop striving to be someone we're not. We stop chasing the illusion that leadership success depends on mastering every skill or meeting every expectation. We learn to see our limitations not as deficits but as part of the design, and an invitation to lead with humility, to partner well, and to build teams that complement our style rather than mirror it.

It's the difference between thinking, *If only I were more* _____ *or I'm not enough,* and instead, *I bring something valuable and essential, even if it's not everything, and that doesn't make me any less capable as a leader.*

When we make peace with what we're not, we create the

mental and emotional space to focus on what we are, and to lead with clarity, compassion, and courage from that place.

Three Limitations of Leaders: What We Lack, Overuse, or Don't See (Yet)

As we continue leading from a place of self-awareness, it's time to get honest about the parts of leadership that don't come as easily. Every leader has areas where tasks feel harder, where energy drains faster, instincts are slower, or outcomes are less consistent. These limitations are not all the same, and understanding their differences is essential to leading wisely.

In the next section, we'll explore three distinct types of limitations that show up in leadership, each with its own set of challenges and opportunities for growth. You may recognize pieces of yourself in all three. The goal here is not to feel discouraged but to begin seeing these areas more clearly, so you can lead from a place that is not only strong but grounded in truth.

Limitation #1: Talent Gaps – What Doesn't Come Naturally

The first kind of limitation we face as leaders is the simplest to name, and often the easiest to ignore: our talent gaps. In my initial coaching sessions, I always ask leaders what they think their weaknesses are. Often, they'll say something like, "I'm not as strategic as I'd like to be," or "I'm not good at organizing and time management." But what they're describing are often talent gaps instead of weaknesses.

Talent gaps are areas where you simply don't have a natural talent. For me, one of those areas is idea generation and creativity. I have never been the most creative person in the room. But this has rarely caused me trouble. Sure, it may have slowed me down from time to time when a task required creativity, but it's not the thing about me that frustrates others or disrupts my leadership.

As a new, young leader, I wasn't as willing to accept my talent gaps as I am now. I can recall getting my feelings hurt when a fellow leader told me that I was "resistant to change and lacking out-of-the-box thinking." Now, I fully own that as a legitimate talent gap. The reason I lack that talent is because of the preexisting talent I do have.

What about you? One helpful question to identify your unique talent gaps is, "What have I never been complimented on?" "What do others rarely ask for my opinion on?" "What kinds of tasks drain me of energy the most?"

Over the years, I read thousands of student evaluations about my teaching style, and I can't recall a single time that a student said, "She's the most innovative and creative professor I've ever had." Now, they mentioned other strengths and weaknesses, but it was clear from their feedback that my talent gap in idea generation wasn't holding me back—it just wasn't one of the tools in my natural toolbox.

Talent gaps aren't weaknesses. They're simply areas outside your natural wiring. You're not necessarily "bad" at them. You're just not naturally inclined toward them. That's important to recognize so you can resource yourself accordingly rather than try to become someone you're not. When we don't acknowledge our talent gaps, we risk overcompensating, misallocating energy, or setting unrealistic expectations for ourselves and others. Trying to push through these areas without awareness can lead to frustration, both for us and for those we lead.

The good news? The solution to our talent gaps is often found in meaningful and strategic partnerships. I've learned to reach out to people in my network who thrive in creativity and rapid idea generation. These are my colleagues and partners who seem to have a new idea every minute, and they help me get to the outcome I need more efficiently. Yes, I *can* generate ideas, and I do. But not at the speed or volume of someone wired that way.

Understanding why certain areas don't come naturally can bring clarity and self-compassion. My thinking patterns are more rooted in structure, systems, and predictability. My brain is built for method and order. Meanwhile, creative thinkers are often operating from an entirely different mental framework. What comes naturally to them often, although not always, means they are more likely to have talent gaps in the areas of my most natural talent. That pumps me up, because it means we need one another to realize team excellence.

And here's something interesting: The things we wish we did better often reveal what we already do well. Our frustrations can be clues. That kind of self-awareness can help you clarify where to direct your energy and where you might need to seek support.

Try using these simple reflections to explore your own talent gaps:

- Because of my natural talent and tendency to _____, I'm less likely to get consistently exceptional outcomes when a task requires _____.

- When faced with tasks that require _____, I often feel drained, avoidant, or unsure, not because I'm incapable, but because it doesn't align with how I naturally think or work.

- I've always admired people who can _____. It feels like second nature to them, while I tend to _____.

Naming your gaps clearly, without shame, makes you a more honest, resourced, and trustworthy leader. Doing this frees you from pretending to be everything so you can show up with clarity about what you are, and aren't, bringing to the table. It also frees others on your team to feel more comfortable exploring and naming their own talent gaps.

Limitation #2: Weaknesses – What Comes a Little Too Naturally

Of course, not every challenge comes from what we don't have. Some of the hardest ones come from the very things we do well—but just a little too much or at the wrong times and places. These are overexpressions or misapplications of our talent. These overuses don't come out of nowhere. They're strengths showing up without boundaries or balance.

Consider these familiar examples:

- The naturally persuasive leader who unknowingly dominates conversations.

- The highly relational manager who avoids conflict to keep the peace.

- The detail-oriented planner who struggles to adapt when things go off-script.

These tendencies aren't random. Many of us have heard the feedback before. The social kid who got in trouble for talking too much? Now he's a team member who struggles to listen. The analytical thinker who asked "Why?" one too many times in school and offended her teachers? Now, she's a leader who can't let a plan move forward an inch without dissecting it. And of course, the interpersonally curious kid who got nicknamed "The Nose"? That's me. If I'm not careful to regulate my talents and strengths, I can still be perceived as nosy and overinvolved. We often downplay these tendencies because they feel like "just who we are." But unrefined strengths can frustrate others, even if they're well-intended. What feels natural to us can feel overwhelming, confusing, or even self-serving to the people around us.

Here's a reflection to carry with you:

What part of you might others perceive as "too much" sometimes—and what strength is fueling that perception? Try filling in the blank with one way that your talent can be misapplied or dialed up too much:

Because I'm _____, sometimes I _____.

Here are a few more examples of what this can sound like in practice:

- Because I'm focused on excellence, sometimes I come across as overly critical or hard to please.

- Because I'm highly independent, sometimes I forget to bring others along with me.

- Because I move quickly, sometimes I leave people behind or skip necessary steps.

- Because I value unity and harmony, sometimes I avoid naming what needs to be said.

- Because I think ten steps ahead, sometimes I forget to clarify what's needed right now.

This exercise builds awareness of how your strengths land with others—and helps you notice when they drift into unproductive territory. When we start seeing these patterns, we gain more power to redirect them. We can learn to adapt our intensity, change our timing, or shift our approach without changing who we are.

The solution to our weaknesses is often found in better

regulation of our talent and strength. Sometimes the thing we think we need to "tone down" is actually exactly what we need to refine (more on this soon). Without regulation, our strengths can overwhelm people instead of illuminating a situation.

Under pressure, that regulation becomes harder. Even when we know our patterns, even when we've done the work to regulate them, stress has a way of breaking through. Pressure turns familiar tendencies into exaggerated reflexes. That's when our strengths stop serving and start sabotaging.

I've seen it in myself and in nearly every leader I've coached. We think we've got a handle on how we show up until something stressful happens. The pace picks up, expectations shift, emotions run high, and suddenly, the strength we've worked so hard to leverage starts working against us.

Stress cranks up the volume on what's already playing in the background. That's why recognizing our stress patterns matters as much as recognizing our strengths. Let's talk about what happens when pressure pushes our strengths to their breaking point.

Stress Patterns: How Pressure Distorts Our Strengths

Even the most self-aware leaders struggle under pressure. Stress, fatigue, and conflict have a way of pulling our strengths into overdrive. What normally serves us can suddenly feel like a trap. We may talk too much, push too hard, avoid too much, or revert to old habits we thought we had moved past.

These aren't signs of failure but signals that our internal resources are running low. The collaborative leader becomes overly accommodating. The visionary tunes out the details. The planner tightens their grip on control. These are our stress patterns, and every one of us has them.

Recognizing these patterns is one of the most powerful ways to prevent our natural style from becoming a source of frustration for ourselves and the people around us. When you can name your stress defaults, you can start to build recovery strategies and support systems that keep your leadership steady, even in the hard moments.

REFLECTION QUESTIONS

When I'm overwhelmed, what version of me tends to show up?

_____

_____

_____

Which of my strengths do I overuse to feel safe or effective?

_____

_____

_____

LIMITATIONS

How do I show up when under-resourced, overwhelmed, or criticized?

_____

_____

_____

How might those patterns affect the people around me?

_____

_____

_____

Stress is inevitable, but being owned by it is not. The goal here is to learn how we respond to stress and lead ourselves well during those times. When we learn to notice these stress patterns, and choose how we show up anyway, we stop letting pressure write the story for us.

When Strengths Go Sideways

In chapter five, we explored a broad set of strengths that often appear in leadership contexts—the natural talents that energize us, shape our impact, and help us lead well. But as we've seen throughout this chapter, even our greatest strengths can backfire when misused, overused, or misunderstood.

This section revisits that same list on pages 124–129, but through a new lens. What happens when those strengths become liabilities? How might others perceive them, and me, when they're not grounded in self-awareness? Use this as a reference point to examine how your best traits might also get in your way and how to bring them back into balance.

Word to the wise. This one can sting a little bit. Keep in mind that this isn't a checklist of flaws but an invitation to see yourself more clearly and to make minor adjustments that have a major impact.

THINKING AND PROBLEM-SOLVING STRENGTHS	
Pattern Recognition	You may see connections and trends so quickly that others feel confused, rushed, or overwhelmed by conclusions they don't yet understand.
Creative Problem-Solving	Your unconventional ideas might be perceived as unrealistic, unfocused, or disconnected from practical constraints.
Logical Structuring	You might become rigid in your thinking, prioritizing logic over nuance, or dismissing emotional input as irrelevant.
Big-Picture Thinking	You may overlook critical details or unintentionally frustrate others who need more structure and concrete steps.
Contextual Awareness	You might become anchored to the past or slow down decision-making by overanalyze historical patterns.
Data-Driven Decision-Making	You may lean so heavily on numbers that you discount intuition, lived experience, or interpersonal dynamics.
Anticipatory Thinking	Others may see you as overly cautious or anxious, especially if you focus too much on hypothetical problems.
Simplification and Synthesis	You might be so focused on clarity and distillation that you miss necessary complexity or nuance.
Curiosity and Inquiry	You may ask so many questions that it feels like doubt, interrogation, or a lack of decisiveness.
Systems Thinking	Your complex mental models may overwhelm others or slow momentum as you try to account for every variable.

PEOPLE AND RELATIONSHIP STRENGTHS	
Connector	You might over-prioritize relationships, leading to blurred boundaries, favoritism, or people-pleasing tendencies.
Motivator	Your energy could come across as inauthentic, performative, or exhausting for those who don't share the same tempo.
Empathetic Listener	You may absorb others' emotions to the point of personal depletion or avoid hard truths to protect feelings.
Talent Spotter	You might see potential where there's no follow-through, which could lead to misplaced trust or unrealistic expectations.
Bridge Builder	Your desire to connect opposing views could result in conflict avoidance or failure to take a clear stance.
Trust Builder	You might hesitate to challenge others or fear disappointing them, putting harmony over accountability.
Personalized Leadership	You could inadvertently create inconsistency or perceptions of favoritism by adapting too much.
Conflict Navigator	You may over-focus on smoothing things over rather than allowing necessary tension to surface and resolve.
Emotional Agility	Your ability to pivot emotionally could confuse others who interpret it as unpredictable or insincere.
Storytelling Influence	You might rely so much on narrative that people question the data, details, or practical application behind your ideas.

LIMITATIONS

EXECUTION AND PRODUCTIVITY STRENGTHS	
Optimizer	You may become overly critical of inefficiencies or frustrate others with constant tweaks and process changes.
Follow-Through	Your commitment to finishing could cause you to cling to outdated plans or resist necessary change.
High Standards	You might unintentionally create pressure, perfectionism, or unrealistic expectations for yourself or your team.
Crisis Clarity	You may unintentionally downplay others' emotions or skip over important reflection in your rush to stabilize.
Proactive Ownership	You might take on too much responsibility, leading to control issues, burnout, or disempowered teams.
Time Maximization	Your efficiency could come across as impatience, inflexibility, or a lack of relational presence.
Resilience and Endurance	You might ignore your limits, model unsustainable work habits, or expect others to "push through."
Operational Precision	Your need for accuracy might slow things down or lead to micromanagement.
Adaptability	You may shift directions too often or struggle to provide consistency and long-term structure.
Resourcefulness	You might overextend yourself or develop workarounds that sacrifice scalability or long-term impact.

COMMUNICATION AND INFLUENCE STRENGTHS	
Persuasive Storytelling	You may over-rely on charisma and narrative, which could lead others to question your objectivity.
Clarity in Complexity	Your drive for simplicity might make others feel you skipped important details or depth.
Presence and Gravitas	You may intimidate or overwhelm others without realizing it, especially in emotionally charged situations.
Adaptable Communication	You might shape-shift so much that others struggle to understand your true position or intentions.
Thought Leadership	You could become detached from everyday operations or dismiss practical feedback that doesn't fit your vision.
Collaboration Catalyst	You might over-involve stakeholders, slowing down decisions or avoiding conflict.
Sensemaking	You may step in too often to clarify or guide, disempowering others from figuring things out themselves.
Diplomacy and Tact	You might hold back hard truths for too long or sugarcoat messages to avoid discomfort.
Constructive Challenger	Your questions could be perceived as combative or critical without trust.
Feedback Champion	You might become overly fixated on growth and critique, even when reassurance or celebration is needed.

INNOVATION AND FUTURE-ORIENTED STRENGTHS

Visionary Thinking	You may be seen as disconnected from present realities or leave others unsure how to act on your ideas.
Risk Assessment	You might overanalyze or delay bold action, caught in "what if" thinking.
Change Agility	You may unintentionally create instability or change fatigue by pivoting too frequently.
Disruptive Thinking	Others might view your ideas as too radical, impractical, or dismissive of tradition.
Opportunity Spotting	You may chase too many options at once, leaving your team unclear on priorities.
Foresight and Trend Awareness	You could become overly focused on what's next, neglecting what's happening right now.
Idea Amplification	You might unintentionally take over or overshadow others' contributions in the process of refining.
Inventiveness	You may be perceived as unfocused or hard to pin down when constant iteration becomes the norm.
Resilient Experimentation	You might celebrate learning from failure while overlooking the costs or consequences of frequent trial and error.
Cross-Disciplinary Thinking	Others may struggle to follow your thinking if it jumps too quickly across domains or lacks a clear throughline.

Do any of those sound familiar? No judgment! Seeing where our strengths might be doing a bit too much and getting curious about what others might be experiencing is the work of congruent leadership. Which ones made you laugh (or cringe) because you've heard it before?

Limitation #3: Blind Spots – What You Don't See but Others Do

If talent gaps are what we don't have and weaknesses are what we sometimes overdo, blind spots are what we can't see but others sure do. They're the unseen of our leadership behavior, often invisible to us until someone gently (or not-so-gently) holds up a mirror.

I've lost count of how many times, in workshops or coaching sessions, I've heard someone say, "I had no idea I was perceived that way" when we're discussing how our talents and strengths show up unproductively. This realization reflects such a common aha moment, and it always makes me think of the Johari Window, a model developed by psychologists Joseph Luft and Harrington Ingham in 1955 to help people better understand their relationships with themselves and others.[30] You'll find the Johari Window in most communication and psychology textbooks. It's a classic for a reason. The Johari Window illustrates the difference between how we see ourselves and how others see us, highlighting the value of feedback in reducing blind spots and deepening trust.

The four quadrants according to the Johari Window are:

1. **Open**: What I know about myself and what others know too.

2. **Hidden**: What I know about myself but others don't.

3. **Blind**: What others know about me but I don't.

4. **Unknown**: What neither I nor others know yet.

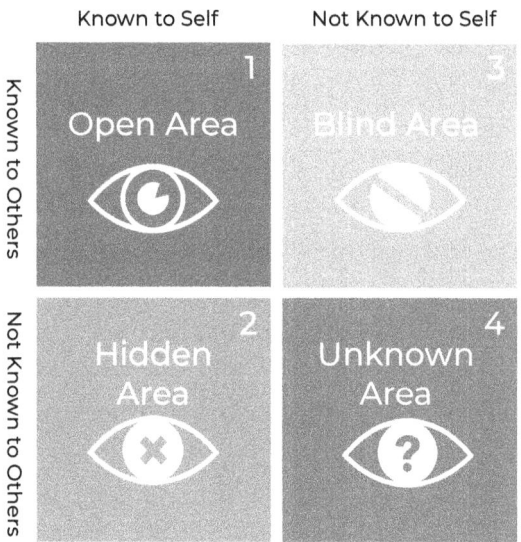

Blind spots are the parts of us that shape our impact but remain outside our awareness. They're not necessarily ill-intentioned. In fact, similar to our known weaknesses, many blind spots stem from underdeveloped, misapplied, or overused strengths. They might also be patterns we've never questioned, ways of communicating, making decisions, or reacting under pressure that feel normal to us but confusing or frustrating to others. These behaviors often feel so "us" that we don't think twice about them, but they're exactly what others may be adapting to, confused by, or quietly working around. That's what makes blind spots so tricky: we often don't know they're there until someone tells us. And by the time someone does, they've already done some damage.

So, are blind spots *different* from weaknesses?

Yes—and no.

Not every blind spot is a weakness. Some blind spots are just unawareness: a habit of interrupting, a harsher-than-intended tone, a tendency to assume consensus that feels dismissive to others. However, once awareness is there and we choose not to do anything about it, it can become a weakness. A discovered blind spot that remains unaddressed stops being innocent. It becomes a willful choice to let it impact others negatively. That's why blind spots are dangerous to our leadership credibility. People care about real impact. And if the gap between what we think we're doing and what others are experiencing gets too wide, trust will erode.

When one of my colleagues told me I was coming across as stubborn to others, I was genuinely surprised. To me, I was just standing in my values with conviction. To them, it felt like I believed my way was the only right way, like the method had somehow become a moral issue. That moment was humbling, but it cracked open a door to greater self-awareness.

One way to shrink your blind spots? Reflect honestly on your strengths. I've seen it repeatedly: When people dig into how their strengths might land with others, the lightbulbs start going off.

- "I always thought of myself as passionate, but I'm starting to see how it might come across as intense or controlling."

- "I thought I was just being efficient, but I'm realizing it felt dismissive to others."

- "I never thought my optimism would make people feel like I wasn't taking their concerns seriously."

When you recognize that your strength has a shadow side, your blind spot starts to shrink. That's the kind of self-awareness that makes leadership congruent, when how you see yourself aligns more closely with how others see you.

Telling Ourselves the Easier Story

Blind spots aren't always things we simply *don't* know. They're often what we don't *want* to know. It's totally human. We all want to feel competent, capable, and good. So when something feels off, our brain gets to work finding the most flattering explanation. We protect ourselves with small, comforting stories that justify our behavior and keep discomfort at bay.

- "I'm just being honest," instead of "I may be shutting people down with my sharp words."
- "I care about quality," instead of "I'm being controlling."
- "I'm driven," instead of "I might be pushing people too hard."

The stories we tell ourselves aren't always untrue, but they're rarely the whole truth. And until we're willing to ask, "What else might be true about how I'm showing up as a leader?" we stay stuck in self-protection instead of stepping into self-awareness.

These half-truths are especially sneaky when they involve our strengths. When a talent starts serving our ego instead of the mission, it becomes a shield, or something we use to feel safe, competent, or in control. These self-serving strengths often go unchecked because they still "work" on the surface.

REFLECTION QUESTIONS

What's a piece of tough feedback I've received more than once, and what personal story have I been telling myself to explain it away?

_____

_____

_____

What's something I've defended about myself that might actually be worth revisiting with curiosity?

_____

_____

_____

When Strengths Become Shields

To us, some blind spots don't feel like weaknesses at all. They feel like our greatest assets. Some of our most persistent blind spots come from our best strengths used for the wrong reasons. We lean on our talents to gain approval, avoid discomfort, or protect our ego. In doing so, we unintentionally build walls between ourselves and others.

These self-serving strengths are tricky to spot because they *still work*. They get results. They reinforce our sense of effectiveness. But they can also leave behind a trail of confusion, disconnection, or mistrust.

If you're not sure whether a strength is serving or shielding, ask yourself:

- Am I using this talent to move something forward or to feel in control?
- In what ways might I be using my talents as shields to protect my ego?

The willingness to ask these questions sharpens your strengths.

A Client's Journey: Reframing What "Giving 100 Percent" Means

One of my clients, an enthusiastic and idea-driven leader, received collective feedback that she tended to overstep in meetings. Her natural strengths made her a confident communicator, but sometimes those same strengths caused others to feel overshadowed or undermined. As we worked together, I helped her recognize how what came most easily to her—her voice, her energy, her quick thinking—could unintentionally create barriers for others. During our coaching call, she expressed concern that if she dialed back her strengths, she wouldn't be "giving 100 percent." But the truth is, using our strengths doesn't typically take us giving 100 percent. Showing up in our strengths is easy! But sometimes, giving 100 percent means regulating those strengths and choosing to pause, listen, adjust, or hold back when needed. And *that's* the harder work. *That* takes us giving 100 percent.

What about you? What would it look like to give 100 percent, not by turning up the volume on your strengths but by tuning and regulating your strengths to fit the moment?

How Old Wounds Become Blind Spots

Sometimes, our blind spots are shaped by what we've lived through. A leader who once felt dismissed may now fight hard to have a voice in every room. Someone who worked under constant pressure might build a team culture that avoids feedback altogether. We sometimes call these *leadership injuries*.

Maybe you were deeply hurt by a leader you trusted, someone who used your vulnerability against you or made you feel small for having ideas. That pain lingers, shaping how you show up, how guarded you are, and how safe it feels to trust others again.

Old wounds often influence how we communicate, how we delegate, and how we respond when things get hard. They can cloud our judgment, harden our posture, or push us into patterns that no longer serve us—or our teams.

Acknowledging what hurt us can give us clarity, help us name what we've carried, recognize what's no longer needed, and lead from a place that's honest, whole, and aware.

What parts of your leadership might still be shaped by pain you haven't unpacked? What reactions or assumptions might be rooted in old stories that deserve your attention now?

Seeing What You Can't See—Yet

We all have blind spots. I've got plenty of my own, to be sure, and so does every leader I've ever worked with. It's part of being human. With the help of the people around us, we can start uncovering what we might not yet see.

- **Ask for specific feedback from people you trust**: Don't wait for performance reviews or conflict to surface patterns. Invite insight regularly. Ask trusted colleagues, "What's something I might not realize about how I come across?" or "What's something you see that I might be missing?" Sometimes you won't recognize a weakness until someone else points it out. Blind spots, by definition, are things you don't see. That's why consistent feedback from trusted colleagues, mentors, or coaches is one of the most powerful tools for growth. We'll discuss this more in the next chapter.

- **Pay attention to repeated patterns**: If different people, in various contexts, give you similar feedback, or respond to you in similar ways, there's likely something there worth exploring.

- **Look at resistance**: Are there parts of your leadership where people tend to disengage, misunderstand, or push back? That resistance may be revealing a disconnect between your intention and your impact.

- **Return to your strengths list**: Revisit the list of strengths from chapter five and ask yourself: "When does this show up productively? When might it come across differently than I intend?"

The more we invite feedback and stay curious about how we're experienced, the more clearly we begin to see ourselves.

That self-awareness deepens trust, sharpens our leadership, and helps us show up with greater intention.

When Leaders Own Their Limitations, Teams Breathe Easier

The way you respond to your own limitations sends a powerful message about what's acceptable and expected within your team.

When leaders are honest about what they're still learning, ask for help without shame, and take ownership of the things that don't come naturally, they create space for others to do the same. This kind of vulnerability, practiced with clarity and intention, builds trust far more effectively than a façade of perfection.

In contrast, when leaders hide or deny their limitations, they unintentionally create a culture of fear, pretense, or perfectionism. Without meaning to, they signal that vulnerability is unsafe, that struggles should be hidden, and growth only happens behind closed doors. People start to mask their own challenges. They hesitate to offer feedback or try something new because the standard seems to be flawlessness.

But a leader who says, "Here's where I need support, and here's what I'm doing about it," sets a powerful precedent, which gives people permission to show up authentically. It normalizes growth, imperfection, and mutual reliance. It fosters a culture where people trust each other, not in spite of their limitations but because of how they handle them.

Your approach to weakness is contagious. You can either pass down shame or model strength through honesty. When you lead yourself with clarity, humility, and compassion in these areas, you're improving your leadership and helping your team breathe a little easier, take more ownership, and trust more deeply.

Workplace cultures shift with one self-aware leader at a time doing the work to create environments where their weaknesses don't get in the way of team success. You don't even have to do this perfectly. With intention as your guide, you can do a good job of creating more self-awareness.

From Self-Awareness to Stewardship: Leading Wisely Through Your Limitations

Once we've done the hard work of identifying what doesn't come naturally, what comes a little too naturally, and what we don't always see, then what?

The next step is stewardship. In this section, we'll explore practical, strengths-based strategies for leading well, despite your limitations, without shame or denial.

Let's talk about how.

Know When Your Weaknesses Are Most Likely to Show Up

Self-awareness begins with pattern recognition. Your weaknesses probably don't show up all the time. They show up in certain conditions, often when you're under pressure, when you're tired, when a task requires thinking that drains you, or when you're triggered by a situation that pokes at your identity. Some patterns stem from how we think, others from how we feel, and both matter when it comes to recognizing when we're at risk of leading reactively. Pay attention to those moments. Start noticing when you're most likely to lean on reactive behaviors instead of intentional ones.

For me, my weaknesses are most likely to show up when

a project starts to go off the rails. Because I value planning and precision, change and chaos often cause me to feel stress and threat, which leads to more rigid thinking and behavior.

REFLECTION QUESTIONS

When do I feel most ineffective or frustrated in my work?

_____

_____

_____

What kinds of tasks make me feel drained instead of energized?

_____

_____

_____

When have I walked away from a situation thinking, *That wasn't my best leadership*?

_____

_____

_____

How you answer these questions can be clues.

Adjust Expectations and Set Yourself Up for Success

Not every leadership challenge requires you to be excellent at everything. It is okay to adjust your expectations to match your wiring. This doesn't mean you stop growing or developing. It means you stop expecting yourself to perform with the same energy and ease in areas outside your natural strengths.

Let's say you're not naturally gifted at details or administrative follow-through. That doesn't mean you abandon those responsibilities altogether, but it may mean you build in tools, processes, and support systems that make the load manageable. Maybe you break your work into shorter sprints or ask for quality control support before delivering a final product. Perhaps you prioritize less and simplify more.

Adjusting your expectations is about being honest about what you can do well and where you need support. Be realistic about what you can own versus what you should offload.

Delegate Intentionally: Surround Yourself with Complementary Strengths

This is where the power of the team shines. One of the most significant benefits of strengths-based leadership is that it helps us see where we need others.

- If you're a visionary thinker, you probably need someone around you who is grounded in execution.

- If you're relationship-driven and collaborative, you may benefit from someone who can challenge groupthink and push toward accountability.

- If you love the messy beginnings of strategy but lose steam during implementation, find someone who thrives on structure and detail.

Delegation reflects wisdom. And it is one of the best gifts you can give your team. Everyone wins when you openly honor others' strengths and create space for them to lead in those spaces. Diversity in strengths and thinking leads to better decision-making.

Let Go of What Doesn't Align—But Don't Use That as a Crutch

Part of managing your weaknesses well is being honest about what drains you and doesn't align with your natural talents. Sometimes, the best move isn't to delegate, systematize, or muscle through, it's to stop doing something altogether. Suppose a responsibility continually pulls you out of your zone of effectiveness and isn't essential to your role or goals. In that case, it's worth asking: "Do I need to keep doing this?"

This is especially important for leaders who find themselves overcommitted or spread too thin. We often hold onto tasks or responsibilities out of habit, obligation, or the belief that no one else can do them as well. But not every task belongs to you. And not every task deserves your energy.

That said, here's the caveat. This isn't an excuse to check out of uncomfortable growth or avoid necessary leadership responsibilities. You can't simply say, "That's not my strength," and walk away from what the role requires. There's a big difference between strategic alignment and avoidance.

The goal is discernment. Know when something is truly a poor fit and can be eliminated or reassigned. Know when something needs to stay on your plate but with better support, structure, or boundaries around it. Strengths-based leadership helps you to show up in sustainable and effective ways.

Leverage Compensatory Tools

You can achieve a good outcome even if something doesn't come naturally to you. Some of the best leaders I know are not naturally great at managing time and staying structured, but they have excellent systems supporting them. They've built compensatory skills that help them manage what doesn't come easily.

Consider tools like time-blocking, checklists, project management platforms, accountability partners, or templated workflows. These systems can reduce the mental burden of trying to remember or muscle through tasks and activities you don't instinctively enjoy or excel at. While you don't have to become excellent at everything, you can become responsible and reliable in those areas by using the right tools.

At times the tools we use to manage our limitations are a little extra creative. I'll never forget when I found my daughter Abby, a social butterfly since birth, sitting on the couch with a piece of tape over her mouth during a movie. When I asked her what in the world was going on, she wrote a matter-of-fact message on a sticky note, "I'm trying to stop yapping." She knew herself well enough to realize that she'd end up narrating the whole plot if she didn't do something about it, so she found a workaround. It wasn't high-tech, but hey, it was effective.

From time-blocking to tech aids to masking tape (apparently), the point is this: You don't have to master everything. But you can build systems—serious or silly—that support your gaps and help you show up well.

Be Transparent About Your Talent Gaps and Weaknesses

One of the most courageous things a leader can say is, "This is something I'm still learning." When you are honest about your growth areas, you create a culture where it is safe to be imperfect. You build what researchers call *psychological safety* (more on this in the next chapter). You're showing your team that imperfection isn't punished and that honesty is valued more than performance. That kind of culture makes it easier for others to be open about what they're still learning too.

But let's be clear. Transparency isn't the same as oversharing. It's not about venting, excusing, or giving up responsibility. Here's a quick list to clarify what transparency is not:

- It's not dumping your insecurities onto the team without a plan.

- It's not making excuses for unproductive behavior.

- It's not over-sharing personal struggles that don't belong in the leadership space.

- It's not offloading responsibility onto others.

Healthy transparency means naming the gap, owning the impact, and actively working toward growth. It means owning your journey and modeling humility. It sounds like, "I'm aware this isn't my strongest area, so I've built in a few supports to help me stay on track," or "If you ever notice I'm doing that thing again, feel free to call it out. I'm working on it."

When you name it, you take the sting out of it. And you show your team what it looks like to grow in public.

Here's what that might sound like in practice:

- "I tend to move quickly, and I'm working on pausing to make sure everyone's aligned. If I start speeding ahead, feel free to flag it."

- "Details aren't where I shine, so I've put some systems in place to help. Let me know if anything needs another look. I won't take it personally."

- "I know I sometimes avoid conflict, and I'm trying to name things more directly. If you ever notice me hesitating, I'm open to feedback."

A few principles that can help you share openly about your weaknesses without undermining your credibility:

- **Keep it brief:** You don't need a confessional. Just a few intentional sentences go a long way.

- **Tie it to action:** Share what you're doing about it, so it's clear you're not offloading responsibility.

- **Create an invitation:** Invite your team to speak into your talent gaps, weaknesses, and blind spots, so they know it's safe to surface problems and questions on their own too.

Talking openly about where we're still growing doesn't make people trust us less. It makes them feel like they can be honest too.

Aim Your Strengths at Your Desired Improvement Areas

One of the most practical ways to manage a weakness is to shift the question. Instead of asking, "How do I fix this part of me?" try asking, "What's the outcome I need and how can my unique strengths help me get there?" This reframing keeps the focus on impact. You don't need to suddenly become detail-oriented, decisive, or comfortable with ambiguity if that's not how you're wired. What you *do* need is a path to the right outcome, and your strengths can help you find it.

Let's say you struggle with organizing a process from scratch, but you're great at asking questions and spotting who's strong in what. Can you use those relational strengths to assemble a team and facilitate a planning conversation?

Or maybe your brain freezes when asked to make a quick call, but you excel at analyzing risks and anticipating downstream effects. Can you use that strength to create a decision framework ahead of time so you're ready when the moment comes?

This is the art of strengths-based regulation. You're not ignoring your limitations; you're actively working around them by aiming your energy, focus, and talents in ways that still get the job done.

It sounds like:

- What outcome does my team need from me right now, and which of my strengths is best suited to get us there?

- If I can't do this part instinctively, what can I do with excellence that still helps move the needle?

- How can I use my strength in _____ to make this task more manageable or effective?

- Is there a strength I can aim at this gap to ensure the outcome still meets the standard?

- What part of this challenge aligns with how I naturally think or work—and how can I start there?

This approach keeps you from trying to become someone else and allows you to bring the best of yourself to every leadership moment.

Here are a few mini case studies of what that looks like in action:

A Leader with Strong Conviction Learns to Soften for Collaboration

Some leaders have a deep sense of conviction. They know what they believe, stand firmly in their values, and bring strong direction and clarity to their teams. At their best, they offer courage and stability in uncertain times.

But the other side of conviction is rigidity. These leaders can become closed off to feedback, resistant to new ideas, or overly dominant in conversations. They may unintentionally shut others down or appear inflexible.

When this leader learns to aim their conviction at the goal of collaboration, things change.

- They use their values clarity to create shared purpose instead of personal agendas.

- They anchor conversations in what matters most but open the "how" to team input.

- They model the strength it takes to pause, listen deeply, and adjust course when needed, proving that flexibility is not weakness but wisdom.

By doing the above, they transform their conviction from something that divides into something that unites.

A Leader with Natural Charisma Learns to Listen for Real Connection

Some leaders have the gift of charisma. They can walk into a room, light it up, and bring energy and inspiration to those around them. Their presence is magnetic and motivating.

But the shadow side of charisma is performative leadership. These leaders can unintentionally dominate conversations, focus too much on being liked, or prioritize style over substance. Team members may feel energized but not truly heard or known.

When this leader learns to aim their charisma at the goal of connection, the dynamic shifts.

- They use their energy not just to inspire, but to draw people in and elevate others' voices.
- They recognize that listening intently and creating space is as powerful as commanding a room.
- They channel their presence toward building trust and not just gaining attention.

This shift allows their charisma to become a spotlight and a mirror reflecting others' worth back to them.

The Bottom Line

When leaders learn to point their strengths inward toward self-regulation, reflection, and intentionality, they don't lose their edge. They become sharper, wiser, and more effective. When you aim your strengths at your vulnerabilities, you refine what makes you powerful in ways that elevate both your impact and your relationships.

Your strengths are tools to help you navigate what doesn't come naturally. You may never become a master of detail or data, but if your strength is in storytelling, you might use that to help others grasp complex ideas. You may never love the ambiguity of change, but if your strength is in structuring systems, you can create clarity for yourself and others even in uncertain environments.

Managing weaknesses doesn't always mean fixing them. Sometimes, it means using what is strong in you to support what is not. That is the art of intentional, self-aware leadership.

Every limitation you navigate with intention becomes a moment of leadership in itself.

Managing Your Limitations Is a Strength

Authentic leadership is found in the ability to see clearly, own what's true about ourselves, and lead wisely despite the things that don't come naturally. When we take responsibility for our impact without shame or ego, we create the kind of congruent leadership that people can trust.

Throughout this chapter, we've explored three distinct kinds of limitations that all leaders face:

- Talent gaps—those areas where we simply aren't wired a certain way.

- Weaknesses—our strengths, overused or misapplied in the wrong context.

- Blind spots—the patterns and perceptions others see, but we often miss.

Each one of these limitations asks something different from us.

- Talent gaps ask us to accept, adapt, and partner wisely.

- Weaknesses ask us to notice our impact and refine how we show up.

- Blind spots ask us to get curious and courageous enough to face feedback we didn't expect.

When we acknowledge and work with these areas rather than hiding from them, we stop leading from fear or habit. We start leading from strength and congruence. We stop striving to be everything and start showing up as someone others can count on.

We'll explore the fifth pillar, Respect the Collective Perception, next. This pillar challenges us to move beyond how we see ourselves and get serious about how others experience us. Because no matter how grounded we are in our own self-awareness, we don't lead in isolation—we lead in relationship. We'll talk about why feedback is one of the greatest gifts a leader can receive, how to move toward it with courage, and what it takes to close the gap between intention and impact.

You've done the work to look inward. Now, it's time to turn outward—to your team, your colleagues, your culture—and ask the question at the heart of congruent leadership:

"How does my leadership actually land with the people I serve?"

MANAGING YOUR LIMITATIONS

Limitation	Definition	Primary Risk	Best Response
Talent Gaps	What I lack naturally	Inefficiency or misalignment	Partner strategically
Weaknesses	What I overuse or misapply	Strengths that create unintended harm	Regulate intentionally
Blind Spots	What I don't see (but others do)	Misperception or broken trust	Invite honest feedback

PILLAR FIVE

PERCEPTIONS

CHAPTER 7

Respect the Collective Perception

Key Question: *What can you learn about yourself through the way others experience and respond to your leadership?*

THIS IS A TRICKY chapter because sometimes, two things can be true at once.

1. **We are not *defined* by what others think of us.** Who we are runs deeper than anyone's opinion, and we shouldn't bow down to the approval of others. That path is a quick way to lose our confidence and become ineffective.

2. **We are responsible for the wake we leave behind when we lead others**—a weighty privilege we should never take for granted.

Our intentions may be grounded in our values, strengths, and integrity, but our impact is filtered through other people's experiences and interpretations. And while we should never hand over our identity to someone else's opinion, we also can't ignore consistent patterns of feedback that follow us from room to room, team to team, role to role. Our teams don't experience our intentions along with our behaviors, tone, presence, and impact. And when there's a gap between what we mean and what they feel, trust begins to die.

You are not who others say you are. But how others experience you still matters. Respecting the collective perception is not about trying to please everyone or believing every opinion about you is correct. It's about being curious. It's about asking, "How do my team members experience my leadership?" and "What impact am I having?" And when we hear tough answers, asking, "What can I own, and how can I learn and grow?"

This pillar invites us to close the gap between self-perception and lived experience, so we can lead with clarity and congruence.

So far, this book has focused inward: motivations, values, strengths. But self-awareness isn't the destination. It's preparation. Pillar Five is the bridge from inner clarity to interpersonal credibility, and it's where internal alignment meets external responsibility.

How Perception Forms

One of the most under appreciated truths in leadership is this: You are being interpreted all the time. Your team is constantly observing, listening, evaluating, and making meaning of your actions, tone, decisions, and even your silence. From the moment you walk into a room, join a Zoom call, or hit "send" on an email, people begin forming impressions of you. Our brains are wired to make meaning. We observe behaviors, assign motives, and fill in gaps with our own assumptions. Over time, those observations coalesce into a narrative, a story people tell themselves (and each other) about what kind of leader you are.

That story becomes your leadership reputation. And whether or not it's accurate, it's real in its consequences, both positive and negative. This is the foundation of *collective perception*: the shared, recurring experience others have of your leadership—not the outliers, but the common throughline across teams, roles, and relationships.

Social psychologists have long studied how we form impressions of others. According to Impression Formation Theory, people make judgments about us based on a combination of:

- First impressions – which are often sticky, difficult to change, and formed quickly

- Consistent behaviors over time – especially those tied to trust, fairness, and competence

- Moments of emotional intensity – especially how we behave under stress or conflict

- Gaps between words and actions – which raise red flags about congruence and authenticity[31]

In short, our brains are wired to seek patterns. So, when your team sees a leader show up with warmth one day and detachment the next or when your words don't quite match your tone, the brain begins filling in the blanks: *Can I trust them? Do they mean what they say? Who are they, really?*

Psychologist Fritz Heider's attribution theory can also instruct us here.[32] People naturally try to explain your behavior. They look for causes: Was it the situation? Your personality? Their assumptions? And over time, they develop stable explanations that shape how they interpret everything you do moving forward. And here's the kicker: Most leaders assume they're being evaluated based on their intentions. But people don't see our intentions. They see our impact, and they create a story based on what they experience, not what we meant.

One kind word doesn't make you empathetic. One burst of frustration doesn't make you toxic. But over time, patterns emerge, and those patterns become *the collective perception*.

Your leadership is not just what you say it is. It's what people believe it to be, based on what they repeatedly experience. That doesn't mean every perception is perfectly fair or complete. But if multiple people across time and context are drawing the same conclusions about your leadership, it's worth asking: *What are they seeing that I might not?*

The only way to truly understand how others experience your leadership is to move toward feedback. Feedback, whether formal or informal, positive or challenging, is the most reliable way to access the collective perception. We cannot respect what we do not take the time to learn, and we cannot grow from what we avoid. That is why self-aware and congruent leaders make a habit of curiosity. They ask questions, invite insight, and listen. Each piece of feedback offers a glimpse into how others are interpreting your leadership, and that understanding becomes the foundation for a stronger impact and deeper trust.

Doesn't this all sound great in theory? The problem is that for most leaders, the collective perception feels like a tidal wave of opinions rushing straight at you.

What Keeps Us from Respecting the Collective Perception

Before we can respect the collective perception, we have to admit that, for most of us, feedback is very scary. Not all the time, of course. Not from every person. But when it really matters, when the stakes feel high, when it touches something close to our identity, when it comes from someone we want to respect us, our brains can go into full-blown threat response. That's our natural wiring.

The human brain is built to protect us. That's basically its number-one job. And in leadership, that protective instinct often backfires. When someone shares feedback, especially if it contradicts how we see ourselves, it feels like danger.

Why? Because our brains aren't great at evaluating feedback with composed objectivity. Nope. Our brains are assessing feedback through the lens of psychological survival:

- Am I still safe?
- Am I still respected?
- Am I still good at what I do?
- Do I still belong here?

To your amygdala, the brain's fear center, tough feedback can feel as threatening as physical danger. You might recognize this as an *amygdala hijack*, a term coined by psychologist Daniel Goleman to describe what happens when our emotional brain takes over our rational brain.[33] In this state, logic goes offline. Our heart rate increases. Our muscles tense. We stop listening. We defend, deflect, or shut down. In other words, we lose access to the very self-awareness that would help us grow and develop.

One of the areas of my work where I see this the most is when I help facilitate leadership reviews or employee surveys. I once debriefed an upward review with a leader who was furious about what his team had shared. He came in angry, arms crossed, and ready to discredit every piece of feedback. He kept saying things like "They're overreacting," "They don't know how hard this job is," and "That's not fair." At first, his responses sounded like pure defensiveness. But as I sat with him and asked a few deeper questions, his tone shifted. He became quiet a moment before saying, "I think I've always been afraid this is how people see me."

The threat to his sense of self was the real threat, and his brain was trying to protect him. What came out as anger was actually fear that some of his worst worries about himself might be true. He had been in a full stress response. But once we named what was really happening, he could stop fighting it and start engaging with it.

I've seen this fear show up in a pattern that might surprise you. It's been my experience that many leaders aren't afraid of feedback because they're arrogant. They're afraid because they've spent years being excellent at most things. Many leaders emerge from roles where they were top performers, high achievers who consistently crushed their KPIs, exceeded every OKR, and hit every metric. They built careers on competence and confidence. They were known for being capable. And now they're in leadership roles where success is no longer measured solely by personal output but by how they influence others. Suddenly, their competence is harder to define. They're managing ambiguity, emotions, and people, so feedback about how they're coming across can feel deeply personal because it *is* personal.

When your success has always been tied to achievement, feedback about your leadership doesn't just feel like a critique of your behavior. It feels like a threat to your identity. And in those moments, it's tempting to let our ego take over. As Brené Brown beautifully explains:

> *Our ego will do almost anything to avoid or minimize the discomfort associated with feeling vulnerable or even being curious because it's too risky. What will people think? What if I learn something unpleasant or uncomfortable about myself? While the ego is powerful and demanding, it's just a tiny part of who we are. The heart is giant in comparison, and its free, wholehearted wisdom can drown out the smallness of needing to be liked.*[34]

No wonder so many leaders avoid feedback. No wonder we brace, minimize, or explain things away. No wonder we fear being "found out" or exposed. But here's the irony: The very thing we fear—being vulnerable, feeling unsure, hearing something hard—is the gateway to real growth. Self-protective leaders stay stuck. Self-aware leaders get better. And yes, it's painful at times. But it's also the path to becoming the kind of leader your team can trust.

Respecting the collective perception doesn't mean believing every piece of feedback is 100 percent accurate. It means noticing when your brain wants to reject something and choosing curiosity instead of defensiveness. It means learning to recognize when you're triggered, when your body tightens, when you start to rationalize or push back, and asking yourself:

- What feels so threatening about this?
- What am I afraid this says about me?
- What might be true here, even if I don't like how it was delivered?

At that moment, you are not just managing feedback. You are managing your nervous system because self-aware leaders don't just hear the hard things. They learn to stay present in the face of them. They regulate the fear response, create sufficient internal safety to stay open, and do the internal work to sort through what is helpful.

One of the most practical ways to do this is to adopt the learning mindset we discussed in chapter three. When we receive hard-to-hear feedback, instead of asking what's wrong with ourselves or others, we can ask what we can learn in this moment. Instead of viewing feedback as a verdict, we view it as data. Instead of feeling attacked, we get curious. That doesn't mean feedback doesn't sting. It often does. But when your goal is to grow, not to protect our egos, we can begin to see feedback as one of the most valuable resources available to us.

Because you can't manage what you don't understand. You can't grow through something you're unwilling to face. And you can't build trust if you only welcome praise. Self-aware, self-regulating leaders know that how you receive feedback is part of your leadership legacy.

At the heart of this resistance lies *cognitive dissonance*: the psychological discomfort we experience when two conflicting beliefs coexist simultaneously.[35] When someone gives us feedback that doesn't match how we see ourselves, our brain kicks into defensive mode. *That's not true*, we think. *They don't get the full picture. They're overreacting.* These internal narratives aren't always wrong, but they are almost always protective. We tell ourselves a story that preserves our self-image and soothes the discomfort.

But self-protective storytelling only takes us so far. If we always explain away the feedback, whether positive or critical, we rob ourselves of the opportunity to grow.

Sometimes, that sting comes because we've overestimated how we're showing up—our intent doesn't match our impact. This is the pain of the overconfident leader, the one who clings to a version of themselves that others don't see. They trust their own story too much and others' stories too little.

But there's another kind of cognitive dissonance: the insecure leader who underestimates themselves. They hear positive feedback and flinch in a different way. *They're just being nice*, they think. *They don't really mean that*. Their actual self is clouded by doubt, and their perceived self—how others experience their presence, contributions, and impact—feels almost impossible to believe. They dismiss praise, downplay success, and quietly wonder when they'll be found out.

Different reactions, same blind spot: a refusal to respect the collective perception about their leadership. One discounts hard truths. The other deflects affirming ones. Both disconnect from reality in a way that erodes trust, both in others and in themselves.

Respecting the collective perception doesn't mean letting others define your identity. It means being brave enough to listen, to ask what might be true in their experience, even when it doesn't match the narrative you're holding. It's not about being shaped by every opinion. It's about being refined by honest insight. That kind of courage makes leaders trustworthy.

Signs You Might Be Self-Deceiving

- **Defensive self-talk**: *They don't understand what I was trying to do. People just don't get how much I care. That's not fair.*

- **Repeated patterns of misunderstanding or disengagement**: If you regularly find yourself thinking, *I have to keep explaining myself* or *They just don't appreciate what I do*, it may be worth asking if there's a gap between your intention and your impact that you're not fully seeing.

- **I'm just being ___ statements that oversimplify your effect on others.** This one sometimes attempts to use your talents and strengths as crutches: *I'm just passionate about excellence* or *I'm just impatient for action.*

These phrases may be true, but they're not the whole truth. When we use them as shields, we stop short of exploring the impact those behaviors may be having on others.

REFLECTION QUESTIONS

What consistent feedback or themes have I heard from multiple people, and how have I responded to them?

_____

_____

_____

What's one piece of feedback I've struggled to accept?

_____

_____

_____

What, if anything, makes it hard for me to trust the collective perception when it reflects something positive about me?

_____

_____

_____

Side Note: When Perception Isn't Just About You

While this chapter emphasizes personal responsibility for how others experience our leadership, it's equally important to acknowledge that perception is not formed in a vacuum. Systems, culture, power dynamics, and bias can all shape the way feedback is given, received, and interpreted.

Leaders may be judged more harshly, scrutinized more closely, or misinterpreted based on deeply ingrained social patterns—factors that go beyond behavior or intent. This doesn't negate the value of self-awareness, but it reminds us that context matters.

If you've received feedback that feels misaligned, ask yourself:

- What parts of this reflect dynamics beyond my control?
- Where might bias or structural inequity be influencing perception?
- What's still within my power to influence with clarity, consistency, and care?

Respecting the collective perception doesn't mean accepting every narrative as true. It means listening deeply, responding wisely, and navigating the tension between personal ownership and systemic complexity.

What It Looks Like When Others Experience You as Self-Aware and Congruent

If you've ever worked with a leader who's truly self-aware, you know what it feels like. Their presence puts people at ease because they are safe and consistent. You don't feel like you're tiptoeing around them or guessing at their intentions. You trust that who they say they are lines up with how they actually show up.

Here's what people tend to notice when they experience a self-aware, congruent leader:

- **They don't flinch at feedback:** Even if it's tough to hear, they don't shut it down or make it unsafe to share. They listen, they reflect, and they own what's true.

- **They show up predictably—not perfectly:** Their team knows what version of them they're getting. No emotional whiplash. No guessing games. That steadiness builds trust.

- **They acknowledge their own impact:** When something doesn't land well, they're willing to explore why. They don't just defend their intent; they get curious about the outcome.

- **They're grounded, not performative:** They're not constantly trying to prove themselves or control how they're seen. Their confidence comes from knowing who they are and not from needing constant validation.

- **They model the behavior they expect:** They don't just *talk* about accountability or openness. They live it, even when it's inconvenient or uncomfortable.

- **They allow others to see them in progress.** They don't pretend to have it all figured out. They're honest about what they're working on, and they welcome others into that process.

If you want others to experience *you* this way, keep going. Everything we've explored so far has laid the foundation. The way you receive and respond to feedback will shape how that congruence is sustained and strengthened over time.

Laying the Groundwork for Honest Feedback

If you want honest feedback, you have to create a climate where it's emotionally safe to tell you the truth. This doesn't happen through a one-time invitation. It's built over time, in small moments that either signal openness or signal that others should be quiet.

Psychological safety is a term first introduced by William Kahn and later expanded upon by Amy Edmondson and refers to the belief that I can take an interpersonal risk—like telling you something hard—without being punished, dismissed, or humiliated for it.[36] If your team doesn't feel that safety, they'll withhold what you most need to hear because they're wired for self-protection too.

Creating this safety starts with you.

- Do you flinch or shut down when someone gives you hard feedback?

- Do you over-explain or defend when things don't land well?

- Do you seek input from others, and actually do something with the feedback?

Even when you think you're being open, your reactions write the rules. Your team is always watching to see if it's really safe to tell the truth. That's why small moments of openness matter so much. The way you respond to a single piece of tough input today determines whether someone will speak up again tomorrow. I once coached a manager who turned a whole team dynamic around just by changing how she responded to one hard comment in a meeting. That small moment of openness gave people permission to be honest again.

Start small. Practice curiosity instead of defensiveness:

- "Tell me more about what you noticed."
- "That's helpful. Thank you for sharing that."
- "I didn't realize that's how it came across. I want to understand it better."

These are micro-moments of trust. Seeds planted that, over time, grow into a culture where feedback is both safe to give and safe to receive. When you normalize those moments, especially in your own leadership, you make feedback less about threat and more about trust. Because nothing says, "You're safe here," like a leader who listens, reflects, and stays present, even when the truth is uncomfortable.

Where to Look: Practical Places to Gather Feedback

You don't have to wait for a formal review to get meaningful feedback. In fact, some of the most valuable insights come from the everyday moments we often overlook. When you train yourself to pay attention and create simple rhythms for seeking feedback, you build a culture where growth becomes the norm.

Here are a few practical places to listen and learn:

Organic Conversations

Most of the time, the best feedback comes from casual conversations. Pay attention to passing comments like "I wasn't sure what you meant in that meeting," or "I thought you were frustrated earlier." These are invitations. Rather than brushing them off, ask: "What made you feel that way?" or "Would you mind sharing more about what you noticed?"

1:1 Check-In Meetings

These check-ins are one of the most consistent and relationally grounded places to gather feedback. Here's a tip. Don't ask big, vague questions like "How am I doing as a leader?" or "What do you think my leadership weaknesses are?" If you ask big questions like this, you'll likely get small, polite answers. Instead, ask "small" focused questions like "What's one thing I could do to support you this week?" or "What's one thing we could do differently during team meetings that would be helpful for you?" When you ask a smaller question, you almost always get a "bigger" answer.

360-Reviews and Leadership Assessments

Whether facilitated by HR or an external coach, 360-degree feedback can provide a more comprehensive view of how you are perceived across various stakeholder groups. These reviews are often anonymized and aggregated, which helps people speak more honestly. The key is how you process it (see earlier section), but the data itself can be transformational. Check out the supplemental online resources at www.TheCongruentLeaderBook.com for a downloadable guide to process a leadership review.

Engagement Surveys and Team Pulse Checks

If your organization conducts regular engagement surveys, request the comments. These open-text responses can reveal what people are feeling but haven't said aloud. Even a team scoring high overall may leave comments that signal deeper issues or emerging patterns.

Coaching and Mentorship Conversations

A trusted coach or mentor can help surface blind spots that your team might feel uncomfortable raising. In coaching, leaders often hear something for the first time that others have noticed for a long time. A mentor who knows your patterns can help you interpret feedback with honesty and clarity.

Exit Interviews and Stay Interviews

People tend to speak more freely when they're on the way out or when you invite them to stay. Stay interviews are an underutilized tool for gathering feedback, especially when framed as a curiosity-driven approach, rather than a performance review. Try asking, "What do you appreciate most about working here?" or "What's one thing I could do differently to make this a better place to work?"

Team Debriefs and Retrospectives

Use project wrap-ups or team offsites to reflect on how things went and not just what got done. Ask questions like, "What worked well about our collaboration?" or "Where did you notice communication breakdowns?"

One more thing to remember: When we ask for feedback, we are not just gathering information. We are also sending a signal to our team members. We're saying, "I'm someone who wants to grow." When we receive that feedback openly, even when it's hard, we model something powerful for the people around us. We show them that feedback can serve as a tool for alignment, a step toward building trust, and a mark of a self-aware, congruent leader.

Mindset Shifts That Make Feedback Work for You

Even the most grounded leaders occasionally get caught off guard by feedback. Maybe it's a comment you didn't expect, a pattern you thought you'd already outgrown, or a review that feels far from the version of yourself you know to be true. When that happens, your first instinct may not be curiosity. It may be something more human: resistance.

Most leaders respond to feedback in one of four ways:

1. **Deflect**: "They don't know me." This is common when you feel confident in your intent and assume others misunderstood. The feedback gets pushed aside, and the mirror never gets a chance to reflect anything real.

2. **Dismiss**: "That's not true." This response can stem from pride or insecurity. Some leaders dismiss critical feedback, while others discount praise because they assume it's exaggerated or undeserved.

3. **Doubt and Shame**: "Maybe I really am the problem. I knew I wasn't good enough." This response doesn't push the feedback away, but it pulls it in too tightly. Instead of evaluating feedback, these leaders internalize it as

evidence they're not good enough. Shame takes over, and self-reflection turns into self-judgment. But just like defensiveness, shame keeps us stuck and unable to grow.

4. **Dig**: "What might be here for me to learn?" This is the posture of a self-aware, congruent leader. Even when feedback stings—or doesn't feel fully accurate—they pause, ask questions, and stay open to what might be true. This response doesn't always come naturally, but it is the most useful. It reflects a growth and learning mindset, which changes the entire frame.

Here are a few mindset shifts that help leaders move from defensiveness to discernment:

- Instead of "This hurts," try "This is uncomfortable because it matters."

- Instead of "They don't see the full picture," try "What part of the picture are they seeing?"

- Instead of "This doesn't feel true," try "Could this feel true to them based on how I'm showing up?"

- Instead of "Maybe I'm just not cut out for this," try "What strengths or support might I need to grow through this?"

This is the posture of a self-aware, congruent leader. Brené Brown says it this way: "I'm brave enough to listen."[37] Even when the feedback stings or doesn't feel entirely accurate, they stay open. They pause. Breathe. Ask questions. They get curious about what might be true and how to grow from it, even if it's uncomfortable.

I once coached a leader who received some tough feedback in a 360 review: Multiple colleagues stated that they perceived him as "not a team player and always fighting for his team over the needs of the organization." At first, he was devastated. "That's not who I am," he told me. "I care deeply about collaboration and the organization as a whole. I just want to make sure my team's needs are represented at the table."

And he wasn't wrong. Mark's team absolutely loved him. They described him as a fierce advocate, a protector, someone who had their back no matter what. However, what we uncovered in our coaching conversations was that this very strength—his loyalty—was being perceived differently by his peers in cross-functional meetings. To his fellow leaders, his commitment to his own team sometimes looked like resistance to shared priorities or unwillingness to compromise.

Once he dug a bit and understood the disconnect, it clicked. "I thought I was being principled," he said. "But I can see how it looked like I was shutting down collaboration across the organization." From that point forward, he didn't stop advocating for his people, but he began to articulate his intentions more clearly. He would say things like, "I want to ensure I'm supporting my team well here, but I also want to find a solution that works for the whole group." It was a small shift in language, but it created a significant shift in perception. And it helped him become not just a strong team advocate but a respected organizational leader.

This story serves as a poignant reminder that the people around us often don't understand our intentions. They experience our behaviors. And when those two things aren't aligned, even good leadership can get misunderstood.

For feedback to become a powerful tool for congruence, you need the right mindset. Without that, even the best-intentioned feedback can feel like a threat instead of a gift.

Earlier in the book, we explored the difference between a fixed mindset ("This is just how I am") and a growth mindset ("I can improve with effort and feedback"). We also discussed the performance mindset (focused on proving yourself) versus the learning mindset (focused on growing). These distinctions become clear in how we respond to feedback.

Which sounds more like your typical response to tough feedback?

	WHAT IS YOUR TYPICAL RESPONSE?	
X	FIXED MINDSET	"This feedback is proof that I'm not cut out for this."
✓	GROWTH MINDSET	"This feedback shows me where I can grow and get better."
X	PERFORMANCE MINDSET	"If I'm a good leader, I shouldn't need this feedback."
✓	LEARNING MINDSET	"Being a good leader *requires* me to be open to feedback."

Leaders who operate from a growth and learning mindset don't get stuck in defensiveness. They listen actively, reflect honestly, and respond intentionally. They've learned how to hear something hard without internalizing shame, and how to mine even imperfect feedback for growth.

After You Receive Feedback

Once we've caught ourselves in a defensive mindset, what comes next is just as important: what we do after the feedback lands. Receiving feedback graciously, especially when it stings or surprises us, is one of the most challenging aspects of leadership. And yet, it's also one of the most important.

But let's be honest: Most of us don't meet feedback with calm curiosity. Especially when the feedback touches something personal, contradicts how we see ourselves, or comes from someone we weren't expecting to hear it from. Our first instinct is rarely, "Oh, how interesting. I'd love to reflect on this!" Instead, we deflect. We dismiss and defend. These tendencies are normal.

I worked with a leader whose team had almost completely disengaged. Turnover was high; trust was low, and the feedback coming in was clear. They didn't feel supported by her. But she was adamant the issue wasn't her. "I've done everything I'm supposed to," she said. "They're just not accountable."

In our early sessions, she couldn't understand why her efforts weren't landing. From her perspective, she was being direct, organized, and results-focused. But her team experienced her as cold, distant, and dismissive. When I helped her see that their perception was a barrier to her success even if she wasn't actually the problem, something shifted. She realized that the team's perceptions influenced how people responded to her whether she agreed with them or not.

That moment allowed us to start doing the real work of examining how her communication and presence might be contributing to the disconnect. Once she took that seriously, we could begin rebuilding trust.

This is the move every congruent leader must learn: When feedback catches us off guard, we can still choose to pause and dig in, rather than deflect or dismiss. Even when it hurts. Especially when it hurts.

Here are a few tips for responding to feedback.

1. First, read or hear the feedback, write the feedback down, walk away, and come back to it later.

2. Let your initial emotions settle. Coming back to the feedback after your nervous system has settled lets you reflect with clarity, not reactivity.

3. Return to the comments with a posture of inquiry rather than judgment. Ask yourself: *What's being said here? What are they trying to tell me? What might be true, even if I disagree with the tone or delivery?*

Another helpful technique is to imagine the feedback is about someone else. Put your researcher hat on and read it as if it were a peer's feedback report. That little bit of emotional distance can help you spot truth without the immediate defensiveness. What patterns do you notice? What questions would you have for this leader? What might you want to ask them about the feedback and their leadership style? What counsel might you offer them to grow and develop?

Sometimes, it helps to talk these ideas through with someone you trust. A peer, mentor, or coach can help you sort what's helpful, what's noise, and what's worth leaning into. One leader I coached told me that her previous director told her once, "You've got a lot of passion for the mission, but you've got to show your team you have a passion for them too." She shared with me about how that one statement helped her understand feedback she'd received for years from her direct reports.

It's also valuable to filter feedback through the lens of your strengths. One of the most useful questions I've seen unlock insight is: "How might this feedback be a reflection of one of my strengths overdone?" Often, our greatest challenges in leadership are simply our best qualities showing up in the wrong context or with the wrong intensity. A pattern of "too much structure" might be your follow-through and planning strength turned rigid. (Again, that one is personal.) A comment about "talking over people" might be your enthusiasm and quick thinking, moving faster than others can process.

That doesn't excuse the impact—it simply provides a more compassionate lens for self-reflection.

Feedback isn't always fun, but it's almost always fruitful. And the leaders who learn to move toward it—thoughtfully, intentionally, and reflectively—are the ones who build the kind of leadership presence that earns trust over time.

REFLECTION QUESTIONS

How might one of my strengths, when overused or misapplied, be contributing to the feedback I've received?

_____

_____

_____

What practices help me create the clarity and emotional space I need to reflect on feedback with discernment?

_____

_____

_____

What About Outlier Feedback?

Every now and then, you'll receive a piece of feedback that seems completely out of left field and doesn't align with the rest of the data or how others typically experience you. It's not the collective perception. It's an outlier. It's tempting to either obsess over it or dismiss it entirely.

Here's a healthier approach: Treat outlier feedback as a data point.

Ask yourself: Is there any context that might explain why this person experienced me differently? Is this a one-time misfire, or have I seen a tiny version of this pattern before? Could this reflect a mismatch of communication styles, values, or expectations?

Sometimes, the feedback reveals more about the other person than about you. Other times, it might uncover a blind spot you hadn't considered. Either way, it's worth holding gently, reflecting on and, if needed, asking a trusted peer or coach to help you process it.

Remember: The collective perception is about patterns and not perfection. Don't let a single voice derail your growth, but don't ignore it completely either. Discernment is the difference between humility and people-pleasing. You're not meant to mold yourself to every opinion, but you are responsible for noticing patterns and learning from them.

Respecting and Honoring Positive Feedback

Not all feedback feels like a gut punch. Sometimes, the hardest kind to receive is the kind that's kind.

If you're a leader who wrestles with self-doubt, you might recognize this pattern: someone gives you positive feedback, thoughtful, sincere, and specific. Your first instinct is probably to shrug it off, downplay it, or silently question their motives. *They're just being nice. They don't see everything. That wasn't a big deal.*

You nod politely, but inside, you're thinking, *If only they knew the full story.* And just like that, the gift doesn't land. It bounces off the wall of your inner critic before it ever has a chance to reach your core. Discounting affirming feedback doesn't make you humble. It makes you unavailable to the truth of your impact and holds you and your team back.

For leaders who carry an inner voice of "not enough," positive feedback can feel unfamiliar or even threatening. It challenges the identity you've quietly clung to—that you have to earn your worth every day, that you're one mistake away from being found out, that your strengths are never quite enough. When someone reflects something good back to you, your brain scrambles to protect that narrative. You brush it off, minimize it, or immediately focus on what still needs improvement.

You don't need to become arrogant to believe people when they say you've made a difference. You don't need to agree with every kind word in full. You do need to practice holding both voices, the inner critic and the outer reflection, and give the latter a little more room to speak.

TRY THIS

☐ **The next time someone offers you positive feedback, pause.** Notice the instinct to dismiss it, and instead say, "Thank you. That means a lot." Later, write the words down. Read them again later. Let the words challenge your assumptions about yourself, even a little.

Let that affirmation become a thread you can hold onto on hard days, when the voice of doubt feels loudest. You don't need to believe every compliment completely. But you can practice considering: What if they're seeing something I've missed?

And maybe that reflection is something you were meant to see too.

Respecting Negative Feedback

It's easy to believe the nice things people say about us—until it isn't.

For many leaders, the opposite challenge shows up: you're confident in your strengths, secure in your intent, maybe even proud of the way you've grown. So, when someone offers feedback that challenges your view of yourself, it feels wrong. Maybe even unfair.

They misread that situation. They don't know the full context. That's not who I am.

Your instinct might be to explain, correct, or file the feedback under *not worth considering*. But if our first reaction to any tough feedback is *that can't be true*, we cut ourselves off from one of the most powerful tools for growth.

Here's what's true: Not all negative feedback is accurate. But most of it is honest. It reflects a real experience, even if the story behind it is incomplete. And whether or not you agree with the full content, the perception itself matters, because your leadership is always experienced, not just intended.

You don't have to take every piece of critical feedback as gospel. However, you do need to be curious about what it might reveal. Instead of asking *"Is this true?"* ask *"What might be true in this?"* That subtle shift can move you from defensiveness to discernment.

You might still decide the feedback doesn't fully reflect your intent. But you might also discover something valuable: a pattern you've been too close to see. A tone you didn't realize was sharp. A habit you've been excusing as personality but that's creating distance with others.

Years ago, in the earliest days of my leadership roles, I received some feedback from team members that caught me off guard. A couple of them shared that they felt I was playing favorites. At first, I was defensive. I thought, *That's not true—I treat everyone fairly. I just happen to have closer relationships with a few team members who go above and beyond, ask for feedback, or show up with a lot of initiative.*

*(Do you hear the "I'm just" response there?)

In my mind, those closer connections made sense. They were the ones who regularly came to me with ideas, asked for coaching, or stepped up in visible ways. But the feedback from my other team members stayed with me. And after the sting wore off, I realized something important: Whether or not I meant to play favorites, some team members felt like I did. And that meant I had work to do to rebuild trust and change the perception.

I started to reflect on how those dynamics might look from the outside. From someone's perspective, it might have seemed like I had a "go-to group"—the people I trusted more, listened to more, or spent more time with. And even if I could justify why that happened, it didn't change how it made others feel.

So, I started to change. I made small adjustments in who I reached out to. I invited more voices into decision-making. I paid attention to who got my best energy and not who earned it from my perspective. Over time, I saw trust begin to rebuild with those who had the courage to share the feedback.

Respecting negative feedback doesn't mean losing your confidence or effectiveness. It means owning your impact. This means saying, "Even if this wasn't what I intended, I'm responsible for how it landed, and what I do next is important."

That experience taught me something I've carried with me ever since: Even when your reasoning makes sense, your patterns still send messages.

Communicating About Feedback with Humility

It's one thing to receive feedback with humility. But how we talk about others' perceptions afterward, especially in front of the people who gave us feedback, can either build trust or subtly erode it.

Some leaders feel the need to over-explain, over-apologize, or over-process feedback out loud. They launch into lengthy justifications, try to clarify what they meant, or turn the moment into a personal monologue. Have you ever given feedback to someone only to regret it because they shame-spiraled? It's the worst!

Others go the opposite direction, shutting down, saying nothing, and pretending it never happened. Neither response models the kind of confident humility we're aiming for.

The most congruent leaders know how to acknowledge feedback with clarity and poise. They own the impact, express appreciation, and articulate a thoughtful next step, without spiraling into shame or defensiveness. Owning something means recognizing its impact and committing to growth. Ruminating means circling the drain of self-judgment without moving forward.

Tasha Eurich, an organizational psychologist and author, makes a helpful distinction here. She writes about how *rumination* masquerades as reflection, but it's really just self-absorption. It sounds like, *Why do I keep messing this up?* or *What's wrong with me?*—questions that focus inward without producing insight. True reflection, on the other hand, sounds like, *What happened there, and what can I learn from it?* This thinking is forward-facing and leads to action.

When you receive feedback that's hard to hear, your next step isn't to apologize profusely every time someone makes eye contact with you. It's not to rehash the moment in every meeting or send a 627-word Slack message about your personal growth plan. It's simply to say something honest and humble, something that signals you heard them, you're taking it seriously, and you're doing the work. For example:

- "Thank you for helping me see that; I didn't realize it landed that way."

- "I've been reflecting on what you shared and thinking about what to adjust moving forward."

- "That's really helpful. I'm sitting with it and working on what that means for how I lead."

These kinds of responses communicate accountability without over-personalizing the feedback. They keep the spotlight on growth and not guilt.

What you're doing here is subtle but powerful: you're showing your team that you take feedback seriously, but you don't fall apart from it. That's what builds psychological safety. That's what teaches others that feedback is normal, valuable, and worth engaging with. You're modeling the message that feedback is part of the rhythm of leadership, and not a referendum on your worth. And when you communicate that way, your team feels your integrity.

As we close this chapter, remember: Respecting the collective perception isn't about surrendering your identity. It's about honoring the lived experiences of those you lead and allowing their insight to shape how you show up. But if we want to lead others well, we can't merely focus on how they experience us—we also have to examine how we experience them. That's where we're headed next. In Pillar Six, See and Lead People as They Are, we'll explore how your own wiring can either distort or clarify the way you perceive the people you lead and you'll learn about practical tools you can use to help your people feel seen and known.

PILLAR SIX

OTHER-AWARENESS

CHAPTER 8

See and Lead People as They Are

Key Question: *How clearly do you see the people you lead—and how can you lead them more effectively by seeing them more accurately?*

A FEW YEARS AGO, I coached a leader who couldn't understand why she kept clashing with one of her team members. "He's just so slow to act," she often said. "I need to work with someone who can think on their feet." I listened intently and then did what any good coach does. I asked some questions to uncover the underlying assumptions present in her thinking. Once we started digging a bit, we discovered something interesting together. Her natural talents were her agile thinking and quick decision-making. She was known for her ability to see the big picture and act decisively. But her team member? He asked questions and studied the details, wanting to ensure things were done right the first time. He brought the most value to the team when he was given ample time to analyze, deliberate, and move forward with thoughtfulness and care. He was wired to slow things down so they could be done right. She was wired to act quickly to avoid stalling. Both of them were bringing something valuable. But because their talents were so different, it was easy for her to see his caution as resistance or even incompetence.

That's the funny thing about perception. We think we're seeing people clearly, but we're actually seeing them through the filter of who we are. Our strengths shape our expectations. Our values influence what we admire. Our biases and blind spots determine what we notice and what we overlook. As Anaïs Nin is often credited with saying, "We do not see things as they are; we see them as we are."

This pillar invites us to confront that reality with honesty and curiosity. This chapter is about perceptual humility and recognizing that, just as we need to understand how others perceive us, we also need to understand the lens through which we perceive others. It's about recognizing how much of what we believe about other people is shaped by our own internal wiring. And it's about learning how to lead with greater accuracy, empathy, and trust by viewing others through a lens of talent, not just your own but theirs as well.

If the last pillar invited us to consider how others perceive us, this one invites us to consider how we perceive them. Together, these two chapters form a kind of relational mirror—helping us examine both sides of the perception equation. Because self-awareness isn't just about how we show up. It's also about how we interpret, respond to, and lead the people around us. Our internal work—knowing our strengths, values, blind spots—doesn't end with insight. It expands into how we view others: the assumptions we carry, the patterns we project, the stories we tell ourselves. This pillar is where the inward journey becomes relational wisdom, giving us the clarity and humility to see people not as reflections of ourselves but as they truly are.

The Power of Feeling Seen

One of the most powerful things a leader can do is see someone clearly, because being seen is a core human need and making others feel seen is a leadership superpower.

When people feel seen, something shifts in the relationship. They don't have to waste energy proving themselves. They don't have to wonder if their efforts are invisible. They don't have to work under the weight of being misunderstood. They can simply show up and do the work, more openly, more honestly, and with more trust.

Consider this: Most employees say they want more recognition at work, but recognition is often a stand-in for something more profound they're craving. What people really want is to feel that their contributions are seen and valued. In fact, author and strengths-based leadership pioneer Marcus Buckingham argues that "people don't need feedback; they need attention."[38]

They want to know someone is paying attention to what they're working hard to offer. That their efforts matter. That they aren't invisible. Recognition that feels generic or routine doesn't fulfill that need. But when it's specific, personal, and grounded in a true understanding of someone's strengths, values, or growth, it builds trust and strengthens relationships. It helps people feel safe, supported, and motivated to keep showing up.

On the flip side, when a person doesn't feel seen, or worse, when they feel misjudged, trust erodes. Sometimes they push harder, trying to prove themselves. Sometimes they pull back, assuming it's not worth the effort. Either way, the disconnect grows. And often, the leader has no idea it's happening.

I once coached a woman named Kara who had been quietly underperforming for a while. Her manager was frustrated.

"She just doesn't seem invested," he told me. "She misses deadlines. She doesn't speak up in meetings. I don't know what to do to turn it around."

But when I met with Kara one-on-one, a completely different story emerged.

She told me about how hard she was working behind the scenes, picking up tasks others dropped, double-checking client details, and staying late to clean up mistakes. But because she wasn't naturally outspoken or flashy, none of that was visible. She'd overheard a comment once that she was "checked out." After that, she felt like no one cared what she had to offer, so she shut down even more.

When her manager finally sat down and asked about her experience, listened without judgment, and acknowledged the value she was quietly bringing, she started speaking up again. Her engagement increased because she felt seen.

Experiences like this reveal something deeper: Our perceptions are often more about us than the person in front of us. And moments like that remind us what leadership really is: not just setting goals or running meetings but tuning in to the people you lead. Learning what matters to them. Paying attention to what they're trying to contribute, even if it doesn't look like how you would do it.

When people feel seen and known, they lean in and trust more. They take more risks, offer more ideas, and reveal more of themselves. And that's what creates the kind of culture where people can thrive.

The Stories We Tell Ourselves About Others

As a leader, one of the most important things you do, often without realizing it, is decide how you see people. You're constantly forming impressions of your team: who's dependable, who's detail-oriented, who brings energy, who drags their feet. These impressions, or labels if we're honest, shape how you assign work, who you trust with stretch opportunities, how you deliver feedback, and how you respond to conflict. Even now, as you read that last sentence, you probably thought of specific people you've led before.

The tricky part is that these impressions don't form in a vacuum. They're created by your brain trying to make meaning quickly and efficiently. You notice someone's tone, energy, responsiveness, or body language and, within milliseconds, your brain fills in the blanks with a story. "She's disengaged." "He's a high performer." "They're difficult." And then, often without revisiting it, that story becomes the lens through which you interpret everything they do.

This *person perception*, while natural, can lead you astray, because your leadership decisions start being driven more by narrative than reality if you're not paying attention.

Person perception is the process by which we form impressions and judgments about the people around us. As humans, our brains are constantly gathering cues—tone of voice, facial expressions, behavior patterns, roles, reputation—and using that information to make quick assumptions about someone's personality, intentions, and reliability. This process is fast, automatic, and often invisible to us. The problem is that person perception isn't always accurate. We tend to fill in gaps with our own expectations, preferences, and past experiences, creating a mental picture of someone that may or may not reflect who they actually are. In leadership, these impressions shape everything from how we communicate to whom we trust, promote, or avoid. That's why congruent leaders don't just trust their first impression or their forty-fifth impression for that matter. Instead, when they find themselves making an attribution about someone they lead, they pause, reflect, and stay curious about the person beyond their current perception.

A director I worked with once described one of her team members as "resistant to change." Every time a new initiative rolled out, this person would raise concerns, ask pointed questions, and seem to slow things down. The leader saw it as negativity. But in a coaching conversation, I asked her what the employee's questions were actually about. She paused and said, "Honestly, she's usually pointing out risks we hadn't considered." What she thought was resistance was actually helping her team prevent failure or groupthink. This team member wasn't fighting the change. Rather, she was protecting the quality of the work. Once the leader realized that, she started inviting this employee into planning conversations earlier. What changed? The perception. The "difficult" behavior became a strength when seen through a clearer lens.

That's the power of story. Your brain is making meaning all the time, and it's not always accurate. The way you see people shapes the way you lead them, and the more honest you are with yourself about the stories you're telling, the more freedom you'll have to rewrite them.

Common Barriers to Accurate Perception

I want us to sit here at this point for a moment, so let's walk through a few mental shortcuts and biases that often show up in leadership and how they can distort our view of the people we lead. If we don't slow down to reflect, these unconscious patterns begin to shape how we treat people, often without us realizing it.

- **The Halo and Horn Effects:** When a team member makes a strong impression in one area, say, being charismatic or analytical, it can overshadow other traits. You may assume they're strong in unrelated areas simply because of that one standout strength. That's the *halo effect*. The opposite happens with the *horn effect*: One frustrating behavior, like interrupting in meetings, leads you to undervalue everything else they bring. Either way, your perception gets lopsided, and the feedback and opportunities you give may not match the full reality of their contribution.[39]

- **Similarity Bias:** Leaders often favor people who remind them of themselves, who work in a similar manner, value the same things, or communicate in a similar way. These team members feel easier to manage and understand. However, when this bias remains unchecked, you risk sidelining individuals who offer valuable perspectives and differences. You might overlook the quiet contributor who needs space to process or misread someone's questioning as resistance when it's really thoughtfulness. Similarity bias limits your ability to recognize and reward the full range of talent on your team.[40]

- **Cultural and Contextual Assumptions:** Leadership doesn't happen in a vacuum. Your cultural background and personal context influence how you interpret others, and theirs influence how they show up. Without awareness, you might misread directness as disrespect, reserve as disengagement, or formality as distance. These assumptions can lead to mismatches in trust, communication, and inclusion.

- **Psychological Projection:** Leadership can amplify the emotions and tensions we carry. Sometimes, the traits that irritate us in others reflect parts of ourselves we haven't fully accepted. If you're struggling with control, you may be more sensitive to someone else's rigidity. If you value speed, a thoughtful processor might frustrate you. This is projection; your reaction may say more about your internal state than the other person's actual behavior. And if you're not aware of it, you'll lead from frustration instead of understanding.

- **Attribution Errors and Confirmation Bias:** When someone on your team drops the ball, are you quick to assume it's a character flaw? ("He doesn't care." "She's unreliable.") But when you make a mistake, do you explain it situationally? ("I had too much on my plate.") That's the *fundamental attribution error*.[41] Add confirmation bias to the mix, the brain's tendency to notice what proves us right, and it's easy to fall into a loop where you stop seeing your team clearly.[42] You start filtering everything through what you already believe, and new behavior doesn't stand a chance to shift your perception.

When I was leading a group of international graduate teaching assistants (GTAs), several were from African countries, including Nigeria, where communication norms are more direct and assertive than those to which many American students are accustomed. I started noticing that some of the undergrads perceived these GTAs as harsh or unfriendly, even commenting as such on course evaluations. In reality, they were simply being clear and confident, which are qualities deeply respected in their home cultures. I had to coach both sides: helping students understand that directness wasn't a lack of care and helping the GTAs adjust their tone slightly for a new context and audience. This was a reminder that what we interpret as personality is often rooted in our culture, and if we're not paying attention, we can easily misjudge someone's intentions.

These biases are not necessarily signs of failure. They are signs that we are human. But when left unchecked, they become barriers to trust, growth, and fairness. Self-aware leaders learn to slow down, question their assumptions, and lead with curiosity instead of conclusion. That's what clears the lens.

REFLECTION QUESTIONS

Who on your team do you find most frustrating right now? What story have you told yourself about why they act that way, and how might that story be incomplete?

_____

_____

_____

Think of a recent decision you made about someone you lead. What assumptions or past impressions might have shaped that decision?

_____

_____

_____

What strengths or values of your own might be influencing how you interpret other people's behavior?

_____

_____

_____

Perception and Its Consequences

Now that we've explored how perception gets distorted, let's look at what happens when that distorted perception drives leadership decisions. As leaders, we are constantly interpreting people and making attributions. And whether we realize it or not, our assumptions about others shape almost everything we do, including how we communicate, make decisions, handle conflict, and even who we gravitate toward and unintentionally overlook.

We tend to think we're being objective because who wants to think of themselves as biased and shortsighted? But perception is shaped by the lens we carry with us, our strengths, values, preferences, lived experiences, cultural norms, and expectations about what "good," "best," or "difficult" looks like.

Sometimes, that lens helps us make quick, intuitive judgments that serve us well. But often, it distorts our view and impacts our developing relationships. We think someone is lazy when they are actually cautious and detail-oriented. We assume someone is checked out when they are overwhelmed and unsure how to ask for help. We label someone as difficult when they are simply wired differently than we are. Here's the kicker: Once we decide how we see someone, our brain starts collecting evidence to support that narrative. It notices the things that confirm our assumptions and filters out the rest.

Psychologists have long studied how impressions form and stick. *Social perception theory* tells us that humans are cognitive misers.[43] We conserve mental energy by making quick judgments and sticking with them. Once a perception is formed, confirmation bias kicks in, and we begin noticing what confirms our original impression while ignoring what doesn't.

Let's look at just a few places this can happen:

- **Communication:** If you assume someone is disengaged, you might start withholding information or stop inviting their input. That dynamic then reinforces what you assumed. You inadvertently create disengagement by the way you treat them.

- **Delegation and Decision-Making:** If you assume someone "isn't ready," you may stop giving them stretch assignments, robbing them of opportunities to grow.

- **Recognition Miss:** You praise one team member repeatedly because they're outgoing and vocal about wins, while another high-performing but introverted team member feels invisible. Your assumption that "they don't need recognition" leads to resentment and eventual disengagement.

- **Conflict Escalation:** You interpret a colleague's pushback as combative or negative, when they're actually motivated by precision and want to avoid sloppy execution. But because their style clashes with yours, you avoid collaboration and miss out on their strengths.

- **Fairness and Favoritism:** Even if you pride yourself on being fair, perception bias can creep in. If you naturally "click" with someone who shares your communication style or background, you might give them more access, more grace, or more influence without meaning to do so. That makes you human. But it also makes self-awareness even more essential.

As a leader, you probably trust your ability to read people. Most leaders do. You've been in plenty of rooms, led plenty of meetings, and made countless decisions about who's ready for what, who's underperforming, who needs support, and who's not quite a fit. You observe, evaluate, and respond. It's part of the job. Yet the research says: We're not as good at reading people as we think.

Study after study shows that performance evaluations are riddled with bias, often unintentionally. We often overestimate the competence of some people based on their charisma or confidence. We undervalue others because they don't operate the way we do. In fact, Gallup once reported that traditional performance reviews are often more reflective of the *rater's* style and mood than the *ratee's* actual performance. Additionally, research from Stanford and MIT has shown that ratings from supervisors are often skewed by factors such as similarity, prior impressions, or the frequency of recent interactions with the person.[44]

In other words, your brain is not a neutral evaluator. It's a meaning-making machine.

We don't see people objectively as we like to think. We see them through our lens, which encompasses our strengths, our personality, values, preferences, background, and our expectations. And unless we're aware of that lens, it's easy to confuse our preferences with the truth.

This is why two leaders can have completely different experiences of the same person. One sees someone who is thoughtful and deliberate. The other sees someone who is slow and disengaged. One sees a team member who challenges assumptions and brings rigor to the process. The other sees someone who is negative and difficult. Both are responding to what they value and how that value is being met, or not.

This is where self-awareness becomes essential. The more clearly we understand our own wiring, the more we can recognize when our perception of someone else might be shaped more by our filters than by their behavior. That awareness helps us pause before labeling someone as difficult or unmotivated. It gives us a pause to ask ourselves a better question about the true nature of the person we are leading.

Seeing Others Through a Talent Lens

When our brains try to make quick sense of people, we often land on traits or labels, such as "difficult, "checked out," or "needy." But what if some of those behaviors are simply talents in raw form?

- A person who asks a lot of questions may be wired for critical thinking.
- Someone who moves slowly might be driven by precision.
- That team member who challenges every decision? They might be deeply committed to excellence or ownership.

By leading through a talent lens, you become curious about the underlying strength trying to show up instead of relying on your (often inaccurate) quick sense of people.

Leading through a talent lens calls for holding people accountable while honoring their individuality and invites us to look beyond labels and see the full person behind the behavior.

To see the potential beneath the pattern, try asking yourself:

- What might be right about what's hard here?
- Is this behavior a clue to a talent I haven't yet tapped into?
- How could I redirect this energy instead of shutting it down?

When you start viewing others this way, you shift from judgment to stewardship. You stop reacting to people's quirks

> and start drawing out their contribution. And that shift changes everything about how people experience your leadership.

Four Practices for Seeing People Clearly

So how do we begin to see our team members more clearly? How do we move beyond assumptions and truly understand the individuals we lead? The next section introduces four practical tools leaders can use to deepen connection and clarity and help your team members feel seen and known: curiosity, presence, self-disclosure, and individualization. Each of these practices helps you pay closer attention to the people around you, build trust, and lead in a way that honors how they are wired. When used with intention, these tools can transform the way people experience your leadership.

Curiosity

One of the most powerful ways to begin seeing others more clearly is by choosing to stay curious instead of certain. Curiosity helps us interrupt the mental shortcuts that lead to bias, generalization, and assumption. It opens a different posture in us, one that slows our judgment and keeps us present long enough to see what's real.

When we approach someone with curiosity, we signal that we're still learning about them. We acknowledge that, even though we have worked with them for years, we still have more to learn.

Leadership coach and author Michael Bungay Stanier describes this practice well. He encourages leaders to "stay curious just a little bit longer."[45] That phrase may sound simple, but it is deceptively difficult. Most of us want to jump to solving, advising, or explaining. But when we stay curious, we give the other person room to reveal more. We begin to see past behavior and into intention. And we begin to notice the conditions they are responding to, not just the actions they are taking.

Curiosity changes the energy in a conversation and creates space where people feel safe to reflect, to offer their perspective, and to name what they need. That safety is what allows people to offer you the raw material you need to individualize your leadership. Because when someone feels seen without being judged, they're far more likely to open up about what motivates them, where they're stuck, or how they want to grow.

The more often you practice this kind of curiosity, the more clarity you gain about yourself, others, and the lens you're leading through.

TRY THIS

- ☐ **Ask One Better Question in Your Next 1:1**: Try asking a question that reveals wiring or motivation. Ask, "What part of your work is most energizing right now?" or "What's something you wish I understood better about how you operate?" These questions invite reflection and open the door to greater self-disclosure.

- ☐ **Replace Assumptions with Questions**: When you find yourself labeling someone as resistant, disengaged, or difficult, pause. Write down three possible questions instead of settling into the story you've already told yourself. For example: "What might be driving this behavior?" or "What could they be protecting or trying to contribute?" Use those questions as a guide in your next interaction.

- ☐ **Practice Silent Curiosity in Meetings**: Pick one person in a group setting and silently observe without interpreting. Notice when they lean in, when they withdraw, and what topics seem to activate them. Jot down your observations as data to explore further, rather than conclusions to act on immediately. Don't creep anyone out though, okay?

Presence

If curiosity opens the door to better questions, presence allows us to truly hear the answers. We cannot truly see people if we are only half-there, physically in the room but mentally already on to the next task or project. Presence is the discipline of slowing down long enough to pay attention. To really listen. To sit with someone, without rushing to label, fix, or redirect.

Author David Brooks writes about this kind of presence in his book *How to Know a Person*, where he describes a posture of "accompaniment." He says, "Accompaniment, in this meaning, is an other-centered way of moving through life. When you're accompanying someone, you're in a state of relaxed awareness—attentive and sensitive and unhurried."[46]

Brooks is talking about more than leadership here, as he's describing a way of being with others that applies across life's roles and relationships. But I think it's a beautiful picture of what great leadership can look like too. Presence shows people that their experience matters enough for your full attention.

But presence is not always deep or serious either. It is just as powerful in moments of laughter, lightness, and shared joy. Playing together, having fun, telling a story, laughing over a team lunch? These are not distractions from real work. They are part of the work of building trust.

Some leaders assume those moments are unimportant, but great leaders know better. They understand that connection builds the safety and context that allows teams to thrive when the stakes are high. Paying attention to people doesn't always require intensity. Sometimes, it just means sharing the moment with them.

When leaders practice presence, they begin to pick up on the subtle signals, like an offhand comment, a drop in energy, or a moment of excitement, that offer insight into what motivates someone or what might be happening beneath the surface. And sometimes, the most powerful leadership move is being someone who truly notices.

TRY THIS

- ☐ **Protect undistracted time with your people:** During 1:1s or check-ins, silence notifications, close your laptop, and give them your full attention. Even fifteen minutes of true presence is more impactful than an hour of divided focus. Your team can feel the difference.

- ☐ **Protect unstructured time with your team:** Laughter, shared meals, and spontaneous conversations aren't distractions from the work. They're the soil where trust grows. Make space for moments that build connection beyond the task list.

Self-Disclosure

One of the most effective ways to understand someone is to let them tell you who they are. But people rarely do that without an invitation.

Self-disclosure is the process of revealing personal thoughts, feelings, and experiences, and it's central to building trust. In interpersonal communication research, *social penetration theory* suggests that relationships develop through a gradual process of disclosure.[47] The deeper the layers, going from surface facts to more personal beliefs and emotions, the more authentic the connection becomes. In leadership, this means that real understanding isn't found in job titles or team bios. It comes from story—shared honestly, received openly, and built over time. Your job as a leader is to create an environment where others feel safe enough to share their stories. That doesn't require long emotional conversations or oversharing and breaking boundaries. It requires thoughtfulness, intention, and good questions.

You can facilitate self-disclosure by asking questions that invite more than surface-level answers:

- "When have you felt most proud of your work here?"
- "What do you wish people understood about you?"
- "What do you need from me when things feel stressful?"

These aren't performance management questions. They're trust questions. Asking these questions consistently sends a powerful signal: Who someone is matters just as much as what they do, and that message is woven into the everyday, not reserved only for performance reviews or team retreats.

> *"I've come to think of questioning as a moral practice. When you are asking a good question, you are adopting a posture of humility. You're confessing that you don't know and you want to learn. You're also honoring a person. We all like to think we are so clever that we can imagine what's going on in another's mind. But the evidence shows that this doesn't work. People are just too different from one another, too complicated, too idiosyncratic."*
> —DAVID BROOKS

People open up when they feel honored—not inspected. Asking good questions is less about getting information and more about giving someone the experience of being seen.

Another way to encourage self-disclosure is by sharing first in small, authentic ways. Talk about how you handle pressure or what motivates you. Mention something you're working on to model openness and not to center yourself. When a leader reflects out loud, it lowers the risk for others to do the same.

And finally, honor what people choose to share. Listen without rushing to respond or interpret. Let their story be the data. The more you treat disclosure as a gift and not a transaction, the more trust you'll build and the more clearly you'll see the person behind the performance.

TRY THIS

- ☐ **Ask open-ended, values-based questions regularly**: Go beyond logistics. Try prompts like "What's something that's felt meaningful to you lately?" or "What helps you feel most supported at work?" These questions invite personal insight without pressure.

- ☐ **Make room for small, human stories**: Set aside a few minutes in meetings or team check-ins to invite personal sharing, like "What's something that made you laugh recently?" or "Tell us one quirky thing about you most people wouldn't guess." These low-stakes stories build psychological safety and connection. When people feel comfortable sharing who they are beyond the job, they're more likely to open up about what drives, challenges, and energizes them at work.

- ☐ **Respond to disclosures with curiosity and care**: When someone shares something personal, your response shapes whether they'll open up again. Instead of jumping in with advice or your own story, slow down and reflect back what you heard. Ask follow-up questions like, "What was that like for you?" or "What made that moment stand out?" This kind of listening communicates that you value their story and are paying attention to both the facts and the meaning behind them. That's what helps people feel seen.

Individualization

Individualization is where everything we've talked about in this chapter comes together. It's the practice that turns curiosity, presence, and self-disclosure into daily leadership behavior. It's the difference between knowing and truly leading someone as they are.

You've probably heard that you should "customize your leadership approach." But that advice often stops short. What does that actually mean? It means paying attention. On purpose. Over time.

That's individualization, and it's the capstone of truly seeing and leading someone as they are. It's where everything you've noticed, heard, and learned from curiosity, presence, and self-disclosure turns into meaningful action. Individualization is the intentional act of adjusting your leadership to fit the person in front of you, not the role you hired them for, not the type you assume them to be, but the real, living, breathing person with strengths, stressors, patterns, preferences, and potential.

Most leaders believe they're good at this. But in reality, we often lead based on generalities. We assume that what motivates one person will motivate another. We assume that everyone wants recognition in the same way, processes information the same way, handles pressure the same way. These assumptions create a gap between the leader's intent and the team member's experience.

Individualization closes that gap.

This practice helps you become a student of your people. It's about taking the time to observe how someone responds to challenges, how they receive feedback, how they light up when given certain responsibilities, or grow quiet in certain dynamics. It's about knowing that leadership is not one-size-fits-all, and that if your job is to bring out the best in others, you have to understand what "best" looks like for them.

Let's say you're working with two high performers. One loves public recognition; the other shrinks from it. If you treat them the same, one will feel energized while the other may feel exposed. Or perhaps one team member needs regular check-ins to stay focused, while another thrives with autonomy and trust. Individualization is what keeps you from assuming one is needy and the other aloof. Instead, you see their patterns, and you lead accordingly.

Here's the truth: Individualization is where self-awareness becomes interpersonal wisdom. It's where your internal work—knowing your own lens, managing your biases, understanding your leadership style—meets the relational maturity to lead others on their terms. It's not only a skill. It's a form of respect. A way of saying, "I see you. I'm paying attention. I want to lead you in a way that helps you thrive." Individualizing starts with a mindset: *I don't fully know this person yet—and I want to.* It continues with behavior: asking thoughtful questions, tracking reactions, noticing energy shifts, and reflecting on what you observe over time. It's the opposite of leading on autopilot. And it builds trust.

People are layered, aren't they? They have patterns, triggers, motivators, and fears. And often, the story you're telling yourself about someone is incomplete at best, and inaccurate at worst. When we think we already know who someone is, we stop paying attention. We miss the little moments that reveal what matters to them. We overlook the clues about how to support, challenge, or communicate with them more effectively.

A senior leader named Ana led a high-performing team yet struggled with turnover among her more junior employees. In her words, "They just don't stick around. I think they want too much handholding." She had written off the pattern as a generational issue. Perhaps you've felt this way before or heard another leader lament the same.

But after a few coaching conversations, Ana decided to try something simple. She started scheduling fifteen-minute weekly check-ins with each of her direct reports. The goal was to ask better questions and listen for patterns.

Within a few weeks, she was stunned by what she learned. One team member felt intimidated by Ana's fast-paced communication style but hadn't known how to bring it up. Another had been quietly taking on too much and was close to burnout. A third had strengths in process improvement that Ana had never tapped into because she had never asked.

Ana realized that she had been leading from assumption, not awareness. And those assumptions were costing her trust, energy, and good people. By individualizing, slowing down, listening up, and staying curious, she was able to re-engage her team and rebuild the kind of culture she actually wanted. The more clearly you understand someone's internal world, the more skillfully you can lead them in the real one.

TRY THIS

- ☐ **Pay attention to patterns**: Every person has a rhythm. Pay attention to how each team member works best. Do they prefer to brainstorm out loud or reflect silently? Do they thrive with clear deadlines or flexible timelines? Do they need structure or space? Start noticing patterns in meetings, one-on-ones, project work, and even their email habits. Document what you observe so you can lead with greater intention over time. Leadership is a study in behavioral patterns. Watch like a researcher. Listen like a coach.

- **Study your team members**: If this person were a system or process you needed to understand to do your job well, what data would you gather? What variables would you track? What feedback would you request? What assumptions would you test?

- **Ask questions that reveal talent and natural wiring**: Build a repertoire of questions that reveal how someone is wired. These questions provide you with real-time data to individualize your approach, and they also foster psychological safety by signaling that you care about their experience.

    - "What kind of environment helps you do your best work?"
    - "How do you prefer to receive feedback?"
    - "What part of your role feels most energizing right now?"
    - "What kind of recognition feels most meaningful to you?"

- **Reflect regularly and recalibrate**: Individualization isn't something you do once. People evolve. Projects change. Relationships deepen. Build in moments to ask, "Is this still working for you?" or "Has anything shifted about what you need from me lately?" These small questions can prevent big misalignment.

Once you begin to individualize, everything changes. You start seeing people less as categories and more as complex, valuable contributors with diverse ways of thinking, processing, and presenting themselves.

This mindset shift should shape how you lead. When you

lead through a clearer lens, you make better decisions about how to support, stretch, challenge, and communicate with your people. You become more intentional, nuanced, and accurate in the way you guide others. Let's walk through a few core areas where this lens makes a meaningful difference.

Feedback Conversations

The way you deliver feedback should reflect how someone receives it. Some people want it direct and to the point. Others need context and care. Some process information right away while others need time to reflect. One leader I worked with realized his quietest team member rarely responded to real-time feedback. At first, he assumed she didn't care. However, when he began providing her with written feedback that allowed her time to respond privately, the insights she shared were thoughtful and deeply engaged. It wasn't resistance. It was a processing style.

Goal-Setting and Accountability

People approach goals differently. Some are driven by outcomes and benchmarks. Others are motivated by a sense of purpose or by people. Some prefer ambitious stretch goals, while others opt for clarity and incremental wins. When you notice someone not responding to the same motivational levers as others, it's worth asking: "How do they define success?" or "What kind of goal structure brings out their best?" A one-size-fits-all approach to accountability leads to confusion or disengagement. But when you set expectations in a way that aligns with how someone operates, you set them up to thrive.

Conflict and Tough Dynamics

When conflict surfaces, the individualized lens helps you slow down and consider: "How might this person be experiencing me?" and "How might their approach be rooted in something good, even if it's frustrating me?" I once coached a leader who clashed constantly with her colleague. She thought he was argumentative and controlling. He thought she was unclear and non-committal. Once they identified the differences, they realized that he thrived in making fast decisions and taking ownership, while she was wired for stakeholder input and alignment. They weren't dysfunctional. They were working from opposite strengths. Recognizing that allowed them to stop fighting and start collaborating.

Recognition and Support

The way one person wants to be seen and supported is rarely the same as other people on your team. One person may light up when they're praised publicly. Another might prefer a handwritten note or quiet moment of appreciation. One team member may value learning opportunities; another may want to crawl in a hole and hide when anyone recognizes them publicly (this is me, by the way!). Recognition is only effective if it's meaningful, and meaning is individual. Ask. Watch. Try different approaches. When you learn what support looks like to someone and deliver it in a way that resonates, trust deepens.

Team Design and Collaboration

When assembling teams or delegating work, think about how people complement each other. Who brings structure? Who brings innovation? Who sees patterns, and who brings energy? A team of high-level thinkers may struggle with execution. A team of implementers might miss the long view. When you lead with an individualized lens, you craft teams intentionally based on strengths and style. When people feel seen for what they bring, collaboration improves.

Leadership doesn't require you to be an expert in psychology, but it does require you to stay curious, to ask more than assume, notice instead of generalize, and to adjust, because you're leading real people.

This All Sounds Great, But...

By now, you might be thinking, *This is lovely for some of my team members, LeAnne. Truly. But what about the people who drive me up the wall and make it very hard to lead them?* You've got someone in mind, don't you? Perhaps you've tried to individualize, ask better questions, and stay curious, and it still feels like a struggle.

This is where all that talk about perceptual humility gets tested. Let's talk about what it means to lead well when the person in front of you is challenging, complex, or still growing in their own self-awareness.

How to Lead a "Challenging Person"

Every leader has someone on their team who feels—how shall we say it?—difficult. Maybe they push back on ideas in ways that feel exhausting. Maybe they're not as relational or responsive as you'd like. Perhaps they always require more information, or they move so quickly that the rest of the team struggles to keep up. Whatever the friction point is, it wears on you.

But here's something we don't often admit: We're probably somebody's challenging person. (If I could put a shrugging emoji here, I would.)

OTHER-AWARENESS

We all have quirks and overused strengths. We all bring certain ways of thinking, processing, and working that don't always mesh well with others. Our blind spots get in the way. Our intensity spills out. Our preferences collide. Before labeling someone else as difficult, it's worth asking what makes that dynamic challenging and what role we're playing in it.

Start here: The person might not be difficult. They might just be different.

Sometimes, your "challenging person" is strong in areas you're not. You move quickly; they slow things down. You ideate; they scrutinize. You focus on the big picture; they want to fix what's under the hood. That tension can be frustrating, but it can also be healthy, if you know how to lead through it.

Sometimes, the person's talent is raw. Their curiosity might manifest as a tendency to question everything. Their drive for excellence might sound like nitpicking. Their desire for ownership might come off as resistance. That behavior may need boundaries, but it also might need development. Some people don't need to be corrected as much as they need to be coached. They need someone to recognize the talent underneath the tension and help them channel it productively.

And sometimes, you're just working from totally different maps. You value clarity; they value creativity. You want to start now; they want time to explore. You build trust through structure; they build trust through freedom. Neither of you is wrong, but when those styles clash, it's easy to misinterpret each other's motives.

I once coached a leader who was ready to put someone on a performance plan. "She just refuses to follow the process," he told me. "It's like she doesn't think the rules apply to her." But as we talked, he described someone with a deep creative drive and strong instincts for problem-solving. She wasn't being defiant. She found the process to be clunky and inefficient. His strength was stability. Hers was innovation. Once he realized that, he stopped demanding strict compliance and started inviting her to help improve the process. The expectations didn't change, but the posture did. That shift created space for collaboration, and the tension became a source of growth instead of a wedge between them.

Not every challenging person is a hidden genius. But every challenging dynamic is an invitation to get curious. To listen harder. To look deeper. And to remember that different doesn't mean difficult, it means there's something to learn.

How to Work with Someone Who Isn't Self-Aware

Let's just say it: Working with someone who lacks self-awareness can be maddening. Whether they dominate conversations, never seem to notice their impact, or blame everyone else for their mistakes, it's exhausting to constantly absorb the consequences of someone else's blind spots.

If you've ever walked out of a meeting wondering how they don't see themselves, you're not alone. These dynamics quietly chip away at trust and collaboration. They confuse teammates. They slow down progress. And they wear on you.

These are common signs that someone is operating with low self-awareness:

- Defensiveness or blame-shifting when they receive feedback
- Lack of reflection on what went wrong or how they contributed
- Tension with teammates or subtle confusion from others about their behavior

- Misalignment between intent and impact, especially when they can't see why people react the way they do

These signs don't mean the person is hopeless. They mean the person is stuck inside their own narrative and hasn't yet developed the skills or the safety to reflect honestly on their impact.

And you can't force someone to become self-aware. Trust me, I have tried. But you can lead in a way that creates space for self-awareness to grow:

- **Focus on observable behaviors, not traits:** Instead of saying, "You come across as arrogant," say, "In the meeting, I noticed you interrupted John three times." Stick to what you observed. This grounds the conversation in something they can't argue with and gives you a starting point for growth.

- **Reflect back the impact calmly and clearly:** Use neutral, specific language: "When you said that, I noticed the room got really quiet. I think people weren't sure how to respond." You're not making assumptions or attacking character. You're holding up a mirror so they can see what others are seeing.

- **Ask open-ended, non-threatening questions:** Avoid statements that feel accusatory. Instead, ask questions that invite reflection and create micro-moments for awareness to grow:
    - "How did you feel that went?"
    - "What do you think their experience was like?"
    - "What were you hoping they'd take away from that conversation?"

- **Help them focus on the perception, not just their intent:** One of the most frustrating aspects of working with someone who lacks self-awareness is that they often fail to accept the feedback. They get stuck defending their intentions instead of facing the reality of their impact. If you try to convince them that the perception is true, the conversation can quickly spiral. Instead, help them understand that the perception is real in its consequences, even if they disagree with it. The goal is to ground them in what's getting in the way of results: "This is how people are experiencing you, and whether or not you agree, that perception is creating challenges." By focusing on the outcome of the perception rather than debating its fairness, you move the conversation toward growth. You're not asking them to change who they are. You're asking them to care enough about their impact to address the patterns holding them back.

- **Create a consistent structure for feedback and reflection:** Self-awareness doesn't usually develop in ambiguity. Use regular check-ins, project debriefs, and shared expectations to create small, structured moments that invite reflection over time.

- **Model the kind of awareness you hope to see from them:** Say things like, "I've been trying to pay attention to how I respond under stress," or "I realized I missed the mark in that meeting; thanks for your patience." When they see you owning your growth without shame, it normalizes reflection and creates safety.

- **Don't expect immediate transformation or make their growth your personal burden:** You may not see progress right away. Self-awareness is a skill, and some people are just beginning to build it. You'll need to be patient but also clear and consistent. Along the way, protect your own mindset. Their defensiveness or blind spots are more about their inner world than about you, so don't absorb it. Above all, stay grounded. Don't escalate when they do. Don't retreat when they shut down. Keep modeling the kind of presence, clarity, and responsibility you want to see.

You can't do their work for them. But you can hold up a mirror with compassion. You can lead in a way that makes it more likely they'll start to see what they haven't been able—or willing—to see yet. In the meantime, you can choose to lead with clarity, kindness, and strength, even when it's hard. And in some cases, when reflection and coaching haven't worked, you may still need to make a hard decision about fit, but you can do so with clarity and compassion, knowing you tried to lead well.

From Perceptual Humility to Lasting Impact

Self-awareness is not complete until it shows up in your relationships. It is one thing to know your values, strengths, and intentions, but your leadership gains real power when you apply that awareness to how you see, understand, and respond to others.

The lens through which you view your team shapes everything: who you trust, how you delegate, when you give feedback, and how you handle tension. Congruent leaders learn to examine that lens. They get curious about their assumptions. They reflect on what frustration might be pointing to. They slow down long enough to notice what they might be missing. This kind of awareness transforms leadership from a one-size-fits-all approach to something more accurate, compassionate, and effective.

Individualizing your leadership and seeing people for who they truly are helps your team feel valued and known. And when people feel known, they are more likely to trust, contribute, and grow.

This is the natural next step of congruence. Everything we've explored so far has laid the groundwork for the final pillar: Own Your Impact and Leadership Legacy. Because how you see others is only part of the story. In the end, what matters most is how your leadership is experienced and remembered.

PILLAR SEVEN

LEGACY

CHAPTER 9

Own Your Impact and Leadership Legacy

Key Question: *How will your daily leadership choices shape the leadership legacy you leave behind?*

WHEN YOU PICKED UP this book, you were stepping into a conversation with yourself, a conversation about who you are, how you show up for your team members, and the impact you leave behind.

If you are here now, it means you stayed with that work. You have spent precious time doing something few people are willing to do: slowing down long enough to reflect, to notice, to grow. That work matters more than you'll ever be able to quantify because it shapes not just the kind of leader you are today but the kind of leader you are becoming.

Congruent leadership brings your inner character and outer impact into harmony and ensures that the story you tell yourself about yourself matches the story others experience. It's about showing up with presence, curiosity, and responsibility—not just once, but over and over again.

Throughout this book, you have explored what it means

to embrace the growth process with courage, to bring your motivations, values, and actions into harmony, to leverage your talents and strengths, to manage your weaknesses and blind spots, to respect the collective perception, and to individualize your leadership by seeing others clearly.

Each of these pillars has been building toward this final step: Pillar Seven, Own Your Impact and Leadership Legacy. Everything you have uncovered about yourself, everything you have practiced in how you see and lead others, has been preparing you for this moment, the moment when your internal growth becomes the foundation for the lasting influence you will leave behind. Keep in mind, though, that this final pillar isn't an outcome you get to in the future but an ongoing practice.

And it starts with how you choose to show up today, tomorrow, and every day after that. That's your leadership legacy.

Leadership Is Legacy in Motion

Legacy is not something you build at the end of your career. It is not reserved for retirement parties, farewell speeches, or written accolades. Your legacy is being shaped every day by the way you show up, the way you lead, and the way you make people feel.

Every moment matters. Every conversation, every decision, every instance of courage or impatience leaves an impression. Over time, those small moments accumulate. They shape how people remember you. They shape whether people feel stronger or weaker because they crossed paths with you.

One thing you might not have picked up about me thus far is that I am a gigantic college sports fan. While my first love is college basketball, I'm also a big-time football fan. In the fall, my Saturday mornings are spent watching ESPN's College Gameday, in which the brightest football minds gather to highlight marquee games, debate who will win, and provide commentary on the sports stories of the week.

In one episode, I had to pause the show to write down a quote from Coach Nick Saban, one of the winningest college football coaches of all time. It was too good not to capture it for a time such as this. While discussing a current story about another leader "losing his team," Coach Saban shared a vulnerable piece of his past that led him to evaluate the legacy he wanted to leave behind.

He said:

> *I think you have a greater chance to lose your team when you're transactional as a leader, which is the way I was until 1998. In other words, everything was about winning or losing. And when we won, I patted people on the back. But when we didn't win, I was probably too harsh, didn't use it as a teaching moment. Negative experiences without teaching kills morale. So, I had to change to being a transformational leader, you know, with somebody who players could emulate—cared about the players for their benefit and not my benefit. You know, had a vision for what we wanted to accomplish and how we were going to do it, and have value-based principles that were going to help them be successful in life.*[48]

When I paused the TV to write this quote down, my two teenage boys were not impressed, but I was. Saban's self-disclosure captured the heart of authentic leadership and transformation. It is not only about how many wins you collect, but about how many lives you help shape for the better.

If you want to build a legacy worth carrying forward, you cannot wait for some future milestone to arrive. You build it now. You build it in the way you listen when it would be easier to dismiss. You build it in the way you give feedback, hold people accountable, show up after mistakes, and navigate conflict. You build it when you choose courage over convenience, presence over distraction, purpose over self-protection.

Your leadership is already leaving a mark. The question is whether it is the mark you intend to leave.

The Leaders Who Shaped You

Before we can fully imagine the legacy we want to leave, it helps to remember the legacy that shaped us.

Take a moment and think about the leaders who changed your life for the better. The ones who saw something in you before you could fully see it yourself. The ones who challenged you when it would have been easier to let you stay where you were. The ones who believed in you when you questioned your own path.

Make a list. Write down their names. Picture their faces. Remember the moments, both big and small, when their influence shifted something inside you.

- Maybe it was a coach who stayed after practice to show you one more time.

- Maybe it was a teacher who handed back a paper with a single encouraging sentence that you never forgot.

- Maybe it was a manager who trusted you with a project that stretched you.

- Maybe it was a mentor who asked you harder questions than you were ready for but stayed to help you wrestle with the answers.

Now look at that list and notice something important. All of the leaders who impacted you the most were not perfect. They all had weaknesses and blind spots. They all made mistakes. They did not always get it right. What made them important in your life was their presence, their intentionality, and the way they chose to lead and live with congruence.

Leadership legacies are built through ordinary moments of extraordinary presence. Through consistency. Through a willingness to care about someone else's growth, even when it is inconvenient. Through the courage to stay connected, even when things got hard or uncomfortable and when walking away would have been easier.

As you think about those people, you begin to understand something more profound about legacy. It is not created at the end of a career. It is created in conversations that could have been rushed but were not. In feedback that could have been sharp but was given with care. In decisions that could have prioritized results over relationships but chose to honor both.

For me, I've been fortunate to learn from many great leaders who cared about me and made me better. My list includes a high school coach who encouraged me to play a bigger game because he saw potential in me, a department chair who coached me back to confidence after several very difficult years, and a leader who taught me how to teach others by the way he taught me.

Even thinking about them for one minute is enough to remind me how weighty a responsibility it is to lead others. They didn't take it lightly, or for granted, and while they weren't perfect, they were authentic, and I trusted them all because of it.

So, here's the deal. Every single one of us, if we're leaders, is already building our legacy. Every day, in every interaction, we are shaping the story someone else will one day tell about us.

The question is, "What do we want our legacy to be?"

Whose List Are You On?

Now, let's turn the reflection outward.

You know the feeling you got when you reflected on those leaders who shaped you?

You have that same opportunity to impact others. Every conversation, every encouragement, every hard but thoughtful decision is shaping the people around you. Leadership is not limited to the projects you finish or the goals you achieve. It is measured in the quiet ways you impact lives, often without even realizing it.

How others experience you is shaping them too. Whether it is the team member who gained confidence because you believed in them, the colleague who learned resilience because you stayed steady during a tough season, or the future leader who will one day model your example, your influence is being written into their lives.

And here's a thought exercise worth exploring. Whose list are you on? Who will remember the way you led, the way you made them feel, the way you challenged and encouraged them when it mattered most?

Leadership invites you to leave more than results behind. It offers you the chance to leave people better than you found them, to shape futures with the way you lead today.

REFLECTION QUESTIONS

Who changed your life by the way they led or lived?

_____

_____

_____

How do you want to be remembered by the people you lead today?

_____

_____

_____

Whose future could be different because you showed up with congruence, courage, and clarity?

_____

_____

_____

Write Your Leadership Eulogy

Several years ago, I heard author and entrepreneur Donald Miller share a practice that was just the coolest. In his book, *Hero on a Mission: A Path to a Meaningful Life*, he shares how he personally wrote a eulogy for himself and reads it regularly to stay anchored to the kind of life and impact he wants to have.[49] Every morning, he reads it to remind himself of the kind of person he wants to be. His eulogy is not about achievements or titles. It is about character, presence, and the lasting impact he hopes to have on the lives of others.

That idea stuck with me, and it challenged me to think about my own life and leadership legacy, not just what I want to accomplish, but how I want to make people feel, what I hope they remember, and the kind of influence I want to leave behind. That is why I invite you to do the same.

Take a few minutes to write your leadership eulogy. Imagine you're at the end of your leadership journey, and the people you have led, supported, challenged, and believed in are reading your leadership eulogy. Imagine them standing together, reflecting on who you were as a leader.

What would you want them to say? What would you hope they carry forward because of how you showed up? Write it down. Make it real. It does not have to be formal or polished. It only needs to be honest.

Once you have written it, schedule a reminder on your calendar to revisit it. You might choose to read it weekly, monthly, or even quarterly. Treat it as a practice of realignment, a way to bring yourself back to your values, your presence, and your impact when the noise of leadership pulls you off course.

I wrote one myself, and I would love to share it with you. And I hope it's true.

A Leadership Eulogy

LeAnne did not lead to be impressive.

She built trust with others through steady presence, honest reflection, and small, consistent choices that shaped every interaction. Her leadership was not loud or self-promoting. It was something people could sense, woven into the way she showed up, the way she listened, and the way she made others feel valued and capable. She knew that leadership was about seeing people clearly, honoring what made them unique, and helping them grow into something even stronger.

LeAnne never stopped asking questions. About herself. About the people she led. About what the next right thing might be. She was not perfect. She did not pretend to be. But she stayed curious, stayed responsible, and stayed committed to leaving every person, every team, and every space better than she found it.

She understood that leadership is not built in speeches or strategy documents. It is built in the way you pause to listen when someone needs to be heard. In the way you ask for feedback, even when it stings. In the way you remember someone's strength when all they can see is their struggle.

LeAnne led with both conviction and kindness. She was strong without needing to prove it. She was humble without minimizing her impact. If you worked with LeAnne, you knew you mattered. You knew your growth mattered. You knew your story mattered. And somehow, because of the way she led, you left believing in yourself just a little more than before.

What about you? Your version will sound different than mine, because *you* are different from me. That is the point. This is not about copying someone else's path. It's about determining how you can best leverage your talents and strengths to leave a lasting legacy and tell a compelling story through your leadership.

You are already writing that story every day. The question now is whether you will write it with intention.

Living the Legacy Now

Your leadership legacy is not a moment you arrive at; it's a journey you embark on. It's a life you're building, one decision, one conversation, one ordinary day at a time. It is not written someday when the work is finished. It is written in the way you show up when no one is watching.

Every time you choose to listen when it would be easier to dismiss, you are shaping it. Every time you encourage instead of criticize, challenge with care instead of shame, correct with hope instead of harshness, you are building it. Every time you take a breath, choose curiosity over judgment, and stay present with someone who needs you, you are writing a story that will last longer than any title or achievement.

Small moments matter. They are not the background noise of leadership. They are the substance of it. They are the reason people will someday say you made them braver, wiser, stronger, or more seen. Or why they will say they never really knew you.

You are already living your legacy. You are shaping it in your words, your presence, your patience, and your courage. You will not always get it right. No leader does. But every time you choose congruence over convenience, every time you lead from who you are instead of who you think you should be, you are building something that will outlast you.

The world is not waiting for perfect leaders. It is waiting for leaders who are brave enough to be real. Leaders who are willing to know themselves fully, to see others clearly, and to own the impact they leave behind. The kind of leadership that lasts does not come from getting every decision right. It comes from choosing presence over perfection. It comes from living with congruence, even when it would be easier to hide behind image or achievement.

That is the journey you have been walking. Every reflection, every uncomfortable question, every moment of deeper honesty has been preparing you for what comes next. You have done the inner work. You have built the foundation that congruent leadership demands—an alignment between your character and your contribution, between your values and your voice.

Now, you get to live it. You get to lead in a way that strengthens others, not just yourself. You get to leave a mark that will outlast titles, roles, and resumes. Your leadership story is being written right now, in the everyday moments no one else sees. It is being built in how you listen, how you respond, how you encourage, how you stretch, how you stay when it would be easier to drift.

You will not be remembered for being flawless. You will be remembered for being faithful to the work of growing, seeing, and showing up. And that kind of legacy is the one that truly lasts.

Thank you for doing the hard, courageous work of leadership. The world needs more leaders like you, leaders who choose to grow, to see themselves clearly, and to show up with intention. Now, go live the legacy you have been building with every small, faithful step.

Notes

1. Ken Royal, "Who's Responsible for Employee Engagement?" *Gallup*, updated November 19, 2024, https://www.gallup.com/workplace/266822/engaged-employees-differently.aspx.

2. Tasha Eurich, "What Self-Awareness Really Is (and How to Cultivate It)," *Harvard Business Review*, published on January 4, 2018, https://hbr.org/2018/01/what-self-awareness-really-is-and-how-to-cultivate-it.

3. Tasha Eurich, *Insight: The Surprising Truth About How Others See Us, How We See Ourselves, and Why the Answers Matter More Than We Think* (Currency, 2018), 3.

4. Shelley Duval and Robert A. Wicklund, *A Theory of Objective Self-Awareness* (Academic Press, 1972).

5. Daniel Goleman, *Emotional Intelligence: Why It Can Matter More Than IQ* (Bantam Books, 1995), 289.

6. Daniel Goleman, *Leadership That Gets Results* (Harvard Business Review Press, 2002).

7. Eva M. Bracht, Fong T. Keng-Highberger, Bruce J. Avolio, and Yiming Huang, "Take a 'Selfie': Examining How Leaders Emerge from Leader Self-Awareness, Self-Leadership, and Self-Efficacy," *Frontiers in Psychology* 12 (2021): 635085, https://doi.org/10.3389/fpsyg.2021.635085.

8. S. Showry and K. V. L. Manasa, "Self-Awareness—Key to Effective Leadership," *IUP Journal of Soft Skills* 8, no. 1 (2014): 15–26.

9. Daniel Goleman, "What Makes a Leader?" *Harvard Business Review* 76, no. 6 (1998): 93–102.

10. James J. Gross and Oliver P. John, "Individual differences in two emotion regulation processes: implications for affect, relationships, and well-being," *Journal of Personality and Social Psychology* 85, no. 2 (August 2003): 348–62, https://doi.org/10.1037/0022-3514.85.2.348.

11. J. Kruger and D. Dunning, "Unskilled and unaware of it: how difficulties in recognizing one's own incompetence lead to inflated self-assessments," *Journal of Personality and Social Psychology* 77, no. 6 (1999): 1121–1134.

12. Erich C. Dierdorff and Robert S. Rubin, "Research: We're Not Very

Self-Aware, Especially at Work," *Harvard Business Review*, March 12, 2015, https://hbr.org/2015/03/research-were-not-very-self-aware-especially-at-work.

13 "Korn Ferry Institute Study Shows Link between Self-Awareness and Company Financial Performance," Korn Ferry, June 15, 2015, https://ir.kornferry.com/news-events/press-releases/detail/488/korn-ferry-institute-study-shows-link-between-self-awareness-and-company-financial-performance.

14 David Stanley, "Congruent Leadership Defined," *JOJ Nurse Health Care* 3, no. 3 (August 2017): 001–002, https://juniperpublishers.com/jojnhc/pdf/JOJNHC.MS.ID.555612.pdf.

15 Sigmund Koch, ed., *Psychology: A Study of a Science. Vol. 3: Formulations of the Person and the Social Context* (McGraw Hill, 1959).

16 Jennifer D. Campbell, Paul D. Trapnell, Steven J. Heine, Ilana M. Katz, Loraine F. Lavallee, and Darrin R. Lehman, "Self-Concept Clarity: Measurement, Personality Correlates, and Cultural Boundaries," *Journal of Personality and Social Psychology* 70, no. 1 (1996): 141–156, https://doi.org/10.1037/0022-3514.70.1.141.

17 Leon Festinger, "A Theory of Social Comparison Processes," *Human Relations* 7, no. 2 (1954): 117–140.

18 Charles H. Cooley, *Human Nature and the Social Order*, rev. ed. (Scribner's, 1902).

19 Carl Rogers, *On Becoming a Person: A Therapist's View on Psychotherapy, Humanistic Psychology, and the Path to Personal Growth* (Houghton Mifflin Company, 1961).

20 Carol Dweck, *Mindset: The New Psychology of Success* (Ballantine Books, 2006, 2016).

21 C. Dweck and E. Leggett, "A social-cognitive approach to motivation and personality," *Psychological Review* 95, no. 2 (1988): 256–273, https://doi.org/10.1037/0033-295X.95.2.256.

22 J. Rotter, "General Principles for a Social Learning Framework of Personality Study." In J.B. Rotter, *Social learning and clinical psychology* (1954): 82–104, Prentice-Hall, Inc. https://doi.org/10.1037/10788-004.

23 D. Nießen, I. Schmidt, K. Groskurth, B. Rammstedt, C.M. Lechner, "The Internal–External Locus of Control Short Scale–4 (IE-4): A comprehensive validation of the English-language adaptation," *PLoS ONE* 17, no. 7 (2022): e0271289, https://doi.org/10.1371/journal.pone.0271289.

24 Eurich, *Insight*, 91.

NOTES

25 Brené Brown, *Dare to Lead: Brave Work. Tough Conversations. Whole Hearts* (Random House, 2018), 158.

26 Edward Deci and Richard Ryan, *Intrinsic Motivation and Self-Determination in Human Behavior* (Plenum Press, 1985).

27 Ben Weidmann, Joseph Vecci, Farah Said, David J. Deming, and Sonia R. Bhalotra, "How Do You Find a Good Manager?" NBER WORKING PAPER SERIES, *National Bureau of Economic Research*, July 2024, https://doi.org/10.3386/w32699.

28 Tom Rath and Barry Conchie, *Strengths Based Leadership: Great Leaders, Teams, and Why People Follow* (Gallup Press, 2008), 2–3.

29 Donald Clifton and James Harter, "Investing in Strengths," *The Gallup Organization*, 2003, https://media.gallup.com/documents/whitepaper--investinginstrengths.pdf.

30 Joseph Luft and Harry Ingham (1955). *The Johari Window: A Graphic Model of Awareness in Interpersonal Relations.* University of California Western Training Laboratory in Group Development.

31 Solomon Asch, "Forming impressions of personality," *The Journal of Abnormal and Social Psychology* 41, no. 3 (1946): 258–290.

32 Fritz Heider, *The Psychology of Interpersonal Relations* (Lawrence Erlbaum Associates, Inc., 1958).

33 Goleman, *Emotional Intelligence*.

34 Brown, *Dare to Lead*, 74.

35 L. Festinger, *A Theory of Cognitive Dissonance* (Stanford University Press, 1957).

36 W.A. Kahn, "Psychological conditions of personal engagement and disengagement at work," *Academy of Management Journal* 33, no. 4 (1990): 692–724 and A. Edmondson, "Psychological safety and learning behavior in work teams," *Administrative Science Quarterly* 44, no. 2 (1999): 350–383.

37 Brown, *Dare to Lead*, 203.

38 Marcus Buckingham and Ashley Goodall, *Nine Lies About Work: A Freethinking Leader's Guide to the Real World* (Harvard Business Review Press, 2019), 116.

39 E.L. Thorndike, "A constant error in psychological ratings," *Journal of Applied Psychology* 4, no. 1 (1920): 25–29.

40 Donn Byrne, *The Attraction Paradigm* (Academic Press, 1971).

41 L. Ross, "The Intuitive Psychologist and His Shortcomings: Distortions in

the Attribution Process," in *Advances in Experimental Social Psychology*, ed. Leonard Berkowitz, vol. 10 (Academic Press, 1977), 173–220.

42 Raymond S. Nickerson, "Confirmation Bias: A Ubiquitous Phenomenon in Many Guises," *Review of General Psychology* 2, no. 2 (1998): 175–220.

43 Asch, "Forming impressions of personality," 258–290.

44 "Re-Engineering Performance Management," *Gallup* (2019).

45 Michael Bungay Stanier, *The Coaching Habit: Say Less, Ask More, and Change the Way You Lead Forever* (Box of Crayons Press, 2016), before title page.

46 David Brooks, *How to Know a Person: The Art of Seeing Others Deeply and Being Deeply Seen* (Random House, 2023), 46.

47 Irwin Altman and Dalmas Taylor, *Social Penetration: The development of interpersonal relationships* (Holt McDougal, 1973).

48 "The Saban Shift: From Transactional to Transformational Leadership," The Daily Coach, October 23, 2024, https://www.thedaily.coach/p/the-saban-shift-from-transactional-to-transformational-leadership?utm_source=chatgpt.com.

49 Donald Miller, *Hero on a Mission: A Path to a Meaningful Life* (HarperCollins Leadership, 2022).

Bibliography

Altman, Irwin, and Dalmas Taylor. *Social Penetration: The development of interpersonal relationships.* Holt McDougal, 1973.

Asch, Solomon. "Forming impressions of personality." *The Journal of Abnormal and Social Psychology* 41, no. 3 (1946): 258–290.

Bracht, Eva M., Fong T. Keng-Highberger, Bruce J. Avolio, and Yiming Huang. "Take a 'Selfie': Examining How Leaders Emerge from Leader Self-Awareness, Self-Leadership, and Self-Efficacy." *Frontiers in Psychology* 12 (2021): 635085. https://doi.org/10.3389/fpsyg.2021.635085.

Brooks, David. *How to Know a Person: The Art of Seeing Others Deeply and Being Deeply Seen.* Random House, 2023.

Brown, Brené. *Dare to Lead: Brave Work. Tough Conversations. Whole Hearts.* Random House, 2018.

Buckingham, Marcus, and Ashley Goodall. *Nine Lies About Work: A Freethinking Leader's Guide to the Real World.* Harvard Business Review Press, 2019.

Byrne, Donn. *The Attraction Paradigm.* Academic Press, 1971.

Campbell, Jennifer D., Paul D. Trapnell, Steven J. Heine, Ilana M. Katz, Loraine F. Lavallee, and Darrin R. Lehman. "Self-Concept Clarity: Measurement, Personality Correlates, and Cultural Boundaries." *Journal of Personality and Social Psychology* 70, no. 1 (1996): 141–156. https://doi.org/10.1037/0022-3514.70.1.141.

Clifton, Donald, and James Harter. "Investing in Strengths." The Gallup Organization, 2003. https://media.gallup.com/documents/whitepaper--investinginstrengths.pdf.

Cooley, Charles H. *Human Nature and the Social Order*, rev. ed. Scribner's, 1902.

Deci, Edward, and Richard Ryan. *Intrinsic Motivation and Self-Determination in Human Behavior.* Plenum Press, 1985.

Dierdorff, Erich C. and Robert S. Rubin. "Research: We're Not Very Self-Aware, Especially at Work." *Harvard Business Review*, March

12, 2015. https://hbr.org/2015/03/research-were-not-very-self-aware-especially-at-work.

Duval, Shelley, and Robert A. Wicklund. *A Theory of Objective Self-Awareness*. Academic Press, 1972.

Dweck, C., and E. Leggett. "A social-cognitive approach to motivation and personality." *Psychological Review* 95, no. 2 (1988): 256–273. https://doi.org/10.1037/0033-295X.95.2.256.

Dweck, Carol. *Mindset: The New Psychology of Success*. Ballantine Books, 2006, 2016.

Eurich, Tasha. *Insight: The Surprising Truth About How Others See Us, How We See Ourselves, and Why the Answers Matter More Than We Think*. Currency, 2018.

Eurich, Tasha. "What Self-Awareness Really Is (and How to Cultivate It)," *Harvard Business Review*. Published on January 4, 2018. https://hbr.org/2018/01/what-self-awareness-really-is-and-how-to-cultivate-it.

Festinger, Leon. *A Theory of Cognitive Dissonance*. Stanford University Press, 1957.

Festinger, Leon. "A Theory of Social Comparison Processes." *Human Relations* 7, no. 2 (1954): 117–140.

Goleman, Daniel. *Emotional Intelligence: Why It Can Matter More Than IQ*. Bantam Books, 1995.

Goleman, Daniel. *Leadership That Gets Results*. Harvard Business Review Press, 2002.

Goleman, Daniel. "What Makes a Leader?" *Harvard Business Review* 76, no. 6 (1998): 93–102.

Gross, James J., and Oliver P. John. "Individual differences in two emotion regulation processes: implications for affect, relationships, and well-being." *Journal of Personality and Social Psychology* 85, no. 2 (August 2003): 348–62. https://doi.org/10.1037/0022-3514.85.2.348.

Heider, Fritz. *The Psychology of Interpersonal Relations*. Lawrence Erlbaum Associates, Inc., 1958.

Kahn, W.A. "Psychological conditions of personal engagement and disengagement at work." *Academy of Management Journal* 33, no. 4 (1990): 692–724 and A. Edmondson. "Psychological safety and learning behavior in work teams." *Administrative Science Quarterly* 44, no. 2 (1999): 350–383.

BIBLIOGRAPHY

Koch, Sigmund, ed. *Psychology: A Study of a Science. Vol. 3: Formulations of the Person and the Social Context.* McGraw Hill, 1959.

"Korn Ferry Institute Study Shows Link between Self-Awareness and Company Financial Performance." Korn Ferry, June 15, 2015. https://ir.kornferry.com/news-events/press-releases/detail/488/korn-ferry-institute-study-shows-link-between-self-awareness-and-company-financial-performance.

Kruger, J., and D. Dunning. "Unskilled and unaware of it: how difficulties in recognizing one's own incompetence lead to inflated self-assessments." *Journal of Personality and Social Psychology* 77, no. 6 (1999): 1121–1134.

Luft, Joseph, and Harry Ingham (1955). *The Johari Window: A Graphic Model of Awareness in Interpersonal Relations.* University of California Western Training Laboratory in Group Development.

Miller, Donald. *Hero on a Mission: A Path to a Meaningful Life.* HarperCollins Leadership, 2022.

Nickerson, Raymond S. "Confirmation Bias: A Ubiquitous Phenomenon in Many Guises." *Review of General Psychology* 2, no. 2 (1998): 175–220.

Nießen, D., I. Schmidt, K. Groskurth, B. Rammstedt, and C.M. Lechner. "The Internal–External Locus of Control Short Scale–4 (IE-4): A comprehensive validation of the English-language adaptation." *PLoS ONE* 17, no. 7 (2022): e0271289. https://doi.org/10.1371/journal.pone.0271289.

Rath, Tom, and Barry Conchie, *Strengths Based Leadership: Great Leaders, Teams, and Why People Follow.* Gallup Press, 2008.

"Re-Engineering Performance Management," *Gallup* (2019).

Rogers, Carl. *On Becoming a Person: A Therapist's View on Psychotherapy, Humanistic Psychology, and the Path to Personal Growth.* Houghton Mifflin Company, 1961.

Ross, L. "The Intuitive Psychologist and His Shortcomings: Distortions in the Attribution Process." In *Advances in Experimental Social Psychology*, edited by Leonard Berkowitz, vol. 10, 173–220. New York: Academic Press, 1977.

Rotter, J. "General Principles for a Social Learning Framework of Personality Study." In *Social learning and clinical psychology*, J.B. Rotter. (1954): 82–104, Prentice-Hall, Inc. https://doi.org/10.1037/10788-004.

Royal, Ken. "Who's Responsible for Employee Engagement?" *Gallup*, updated November 19, 2024. https://www.gallup.com/workplace/266822/engaged-employees-differently.aspx.

Showry, S., and K. V. L. Manasa. "Self-Awareness—Key to Effective Leadership." *IUP Journal of Soft Skills* 8, no. 1 (2014): 15–26.

Stanier, Michael Bungay. *The Coaching Habit: Say Less, Ask More, and Change the Way You Lead Forever.* Box of Crayons Press, 2016.

Stanley, David. "Congruent Leadership Defined." *JOJ Nurse Health Care* 3, no. 3 (August 2017): 001–002. https://juniperpublishers.com/jojnhc/pdf/JOJNHC.MS.ID.555612.pdf.

"The Saban Shift: From Transactional to Transformational Leadership." The Daily Coach, October 23, 2024. https://www.thedaily.coach/p/the-saban-shift-from-transactional-to-transformational-leadership?utm_source=chatgpt.com.

Thorndike, E. L. "A constant error in psychological ratings." *Journal of Applied Psychology* 4, no. 1 (1920): 25–29.

Weidmann, Ben, Joseph Vecci, Farah Said, David J. Deming, and Sonia R. Bhalotra. "How Do You Find a Good Manager?" NBER WORKING PAPER SERIES. *National Bureau of Economic Research*, July 2024. https://doi.org/10.3386/w32699.

Acknowledgments

Writing a book is a strange and wonderful experience: deeply personal, wildly challenging, and almost always fueled by the people who believe in you even when you're not so sure about yourself.

To my clients and students: Thank you for being the inspiration behind so much of this work. Your honesty, courage, and willingness to wrestle with hard questions have shaped me more than you know. I carry your stories with me, and it's been an honor to walk alongside you.

To my husband, Ben, and our kiddos: Thank you for cheering me on with patience, love, and grace during the long writing process. Isaac, Eli, and Abby: You are the best parts of my leadership and life story. I hope you always know that your voice matters, that growth is worth pursuing, and that leading well starts with knowing who you are. Watching you become who you're meant to be is the greatest joy of my life.

To my parents: Thank you for being my first and most faithful cheerleaders. Mom, thank you for laminating and binding my childhood books as if they were bestsellers. Dad, thank you for always making me feel like I could take on the world.

To Viv and Maggi: Thank you for helping create the margin I needed to write. Your support behind the scenes made it possible to bring this to life, and I'm so grateful for your excellence, your encouragement, and your presence.

To Deb, Becky, and Vanessa: Your gifts as coach and editor, designer, and proofreader turned my chaotic and scattered thoughts into something meaningful. Thank you for your wisdom, care, and the many ways you helped me find clarity, voice, and rhythm when I was deep in the weeds.

To Courtney, Meg, Joy, Kenneth, Kerry, Karen, Sarah, and Melody: When I was sure I didn't have it in me, you were the very best friends. You asked, nudged, reminded, and believed, long before I did. Thank you for listening to me process (and, let's be honest, shame spiral), for cheering me on, and for gently reminding me, over and over, that I could do this. Your belief meant more than you know.

Above all, may God be glorified. He placed this dream in my heart, and in His kindness, surrounded me with people who helped bring it to life. This book is a reflection of His faithfulness and of the many voices He used to shape mine along the way.

—*LeAnne Lagasse*

About the Author

LEANNE LAGASSE HAS SPENT her career helping leaders see themselves more clearly, build trust, and strengthen team performance. Drawing on her background in communication, psychology, business, and strengths-based development, she equips leaders to grow in self-awareness so they can align intention with impact and create people-centered workplaces that deliver real results.

In addition to her consulting and coaching work, LeAnne has served as a faculty member at Texas Tech University and currently teaches MBA courses for Missouri State University, where she equips future leaders with practical skills for communication, self-awareness, and organizational success.

LeAnne is a Gallup-Certified Strengths Coach and holds the SHRM-SCP credential, the Society for Human Resource Management's highest level of certification for HR professionals. These distinctions reflect her deep expertise in helping leaders and organizations unlock potential through both strengths-based development and people-centered practices.

As the founder of LeAnne Lagasse Coaching and Consulting, she partners with organizations across industries through executive coaching, team workshops, leadership programs, and keynote speaking. She has guided leaders at every level, from emerging managers to seasoned executives, toward greater clarity, confidence, and congruence in their leadership.

Beyond her professional work, LeAnne treasures time with her husband, Ben, and their three children—Isaac, Eli, and Abby.

Learn more at leannelagasse.com.

Bring Congruent Leadership to Your Organization

You've taken the first step by investing in your own leadership through *The Congruent Leader*. Now imagine the impact when these same principles take root across your team and organization.

This is the work I do every single day—helping leaders and organizations put these principles into action in ways that inspire growth, strengthen teams, and drive employee engagement and retention.

So if you're ready to bring this growth to your workplace, here are a few ways we can work together:

- Keynotes that inspire and energize audiences with practical, strengths-based leadership strategies.

- Workshops and retreats that build trust, improve communication, and create high-performing and cohesive teams.

- Leadership development programs that equip leaders at every level, creating alignment, clarity, and congruence across your organization.

- Executive leadership coaching that provides personalized guidance to help leaders navigate challenges, accelerate growth, and maximize their impact.

To explore keynotes, workshops, programs, or coaching for your organization, visit leannelagasse.com.

And don't forget to sign up for my newsletter at leannelagasse.com/newsletter. You'll receive practical tools, fresh insights, and encouragement for your leadership journey.

~

What My Clients Are Saying:

"Working with LeAnne was an absolute pleasure. Her speaking style is incredibly fluent and easy to comprehend, making every interaction engaging and insightful. She brings both professionalism and warmth to every session, making collaboration seamless and enjoyable."

—SAMANTHA S.

"LeAnne spoke at our annual Summit, and her session was a fan favorite. Throughout her presentation, LeAnne engaged the audience and made her content dynamic and easy to absorb. We've received nothing but positive remarks about her session! She takes incredible pride in her work, and it shows."

—CARLY E.

"LeAnne's passion and dedication to her work radiate from all that she does and is infectious to those she works with and for. Her generosity and kind-hearted spirit are also qualities that set her apart from anyone else. She truly cares about people, and it's a quality that can be felt from the moment you meet her."

—CHELLE H.

www.ingramcontent.com/pod-product-compliance
Lightning Source LLC
Chambersburg PA
CBHW070614030426
42337CB00020B/3793